Presentation
Magic

Dazzle & Deliver
Talks With
Confidence

Marisa D'Vari

Deg.Com International
www.deg.com

Presentation Magic

"*Presentation Magic* is a **practical, easy to read** and thorough guide to excellent presentations that covers **all aspects of giving a speech.**"

Susan RoAne, Author *How To Work a Room* and several other books, Keynote Speaker

"In a brief period the **reader is transformed** from adequate to **exceptional in terms of speaking philosophy, preparation, style, and delivery.**"

Alan Weiss, Ph.D., author, *Money Talks: How to Make A Million As A Speaker*

"An **absolutely outstanding book** for anyone who wants to **speak to and connect with audiences** — with power, persuasion, and impact. Loaded with insightful and helpful tips!"

Nido Qubein, Chairman, Great Harvest Bread
& Co-Founder, National Speakers Foundation

"*Presentation Magic* will *ignite your message, invigorate your audience* and *turbo charge your speaking career* into a *Profit Zone* you've never before imagined."

Tami DePalma, Author, *Maximum Exposure Marketing System*, MarketAbility.com

"*Presentation Magic* **is two years worth of finishing school**, in a package, including **lessons and homework to hone your skills.**"

Eva Rosenberg, MBA, Noted financial and Internet speaker

"Magic comes from pondering, preparation and practice. D'Vari **coaches you** toward creating your own presentation magic."

Patricia J. Bell, author, The *Pre-publishing Handbook*

"Marisa has developed the **primer for anyone looking to develop their presentation skills and confidence level.** Chapter after chapter is a step ladder to success for the beginner speaker."
Vicki Donlan, Founder and CEO of Women's Business

"**Required reading for my sales team.** D'Vari's **fast-paced,** no-nononsense book is most appealing to busy sales people, **helping them make more powerful presentations & close sales!**"
Robin Bartlett, Director of Sales and Corporate Relations
American College of Physicians

"Get set for **fresh ideas** on communication skills and excellent 'assignments' at the end of each chapter that really **drive the lessons home.**"
Marcia Yudkin, author *Six Steps to Free Publicity, Smart Speaking,* and 9 Other Books

"*Presentation Magic* offers those who read it a **blueprint for taking their presentation skills** to the next level. I highly recommend it."
Robert E. Frare, Author, *Partner Selling*

"I coach CEOs for a living, and think **poor presentation skills are epidemic in the corporate world.** D'Vari's *Presentation Magic* goes much deeper than any books I've read."
Darren LaCroix, Toastmaster World Champion, 2001

"This **practical, highly informative** book is full of useful and immediately implementable ideas."
Landy Chase, MBA, CSE, CSP, National sales trainer, speaker & columnist

"Presentation Magic gives you the **information and inspiration** you need to deliver a polished, professional performance."
Rosemary Ellen Guiley, Ph.D, Author, *Breakthrough Intuition*

Presentation Magic

Published 2003
Deg.Com International Publishing
220 Boylston Street
Boston, MA 02116
Email publisher@deg.com
http://www.deg.com
(617) 451-9914

Part of the Speaking Geeks™ Series
of Books, CD's, & Audio Products

Cover Design by Nikki Kramer
Interior Layout by Jason Sands

Dedication

To Ron D'Vari, great looks, dazzling brilliance, and a magical, charismatic presence when presenting.

With Appreciation ...

To **Nido Qubein**, former past president of the National Speakers Association (NSA) for leading a generation of speakers and presenters into the basics of clear communication and underscoring that the most powerful element of a presentation is making an emotional connection with your audience.

To **Tracy Day**, brilliantly skilled at getting to the core of a manuscript and bringing out its essence. Tracy's unflagging dedication to this series is much appreciated.

Once again to **Ron D'Vari**, best friend, co-presenter, and spiritual muse!

About the Author

Marisa D'Vari

Marisa D'Vari is founder of Deg.Com Communications, a leader in presentation skills and media training celebrating its 10th anniversary in 2004.

Deg.Com Communications training provides a safe, supportive environment for personal growth. D'Vari's wealth of experience as a TV talk show host and former entertainment industry executive is what distinguishes Deg.Com Communications in the industry.

To engage Marisa D'Vari as a consultant or to speak at your conference, please email her at mdvari@deg.com or call 617 451 9914.

MEMBER

NATIONAL
SPEAKERS
ASSOCIATION

Marisa D'Vari
Deg.Com Communications
220 Boylston Street
Boston, MA 02116
617 451-9914 Phone
617 351-2030 Fax
mdvari@deg.com
http://www.deg.com

Preface

This book is all about you!

Whether your objective is to deliver dazzling sales presentations in the boardroom, give mesmerizing public talks to promote your book or service, or persuade others of your value, this book contains the tools you need.

Please consider me your coach and muse, introducing you to presentation techniques to enhance your credibility.

I'll be here every step of the way to help you:

▸ Speak with confidence;

▸ Conquer your anxiety;

▸ Connect with attendees;

▸ Discover the power of gestures;

▸ Motivate your audience;

▸ Reinforce your image;

▸ Understand communication styles --

And much more!

CONTENTS

Chapter 1..11
Introduction to Presentation Skills Success
Establishing "Brand You"
Controlling Perceptions
Secrets of Successful Presenters

Chapter 2..17
Crafting a Dynamic First Impression
How Others Perceive You
Mastering First Impressions
Creating Your Personal Image

Chapter 3..35
Understanding Communication Styles
Introduction to Styles
Identifying Your Style
Identifying Styles of Others

Chapter 4..43
Preparing to Present
Confident Presentation Skills
How to Conquer Anxiety
Power of Visualization

Chapter 5..61
Presentation Tips, Tools, & Techniques
Easy Presentation Templates
Turning Prospects into Clients
Enhancing Your Image with Colleagues

Chapter 6..77
Creating a Public Talk
How to Structure the Talk
How to Motivate Your Audience
The Power of Stories and Anecdotes

Chapter 7.. 91
Connecting with Your Audience
Why an Emotional Connection is Key
Effective Eye Contact and Gestures
The Power of the Pause

Chapter 8..107
Successful Presentations
How to Enhance Audience Retention
PowerPoint Secrets
Practicing with Visual Aids

Chapter 9..117
Networking with Confidence
Networking Etiquette
Building Successful Relationships
How to Generate Referrals

Chapter 10..133
Video Conference Success
Preparing for Video Conferencing
Dressing for Video Conferencing
Vocal Secrets for Video Conferencing

Presentation Magic

Chapter 1
Introduction to Presentation Skills Success

In This Chapter You Will Learn

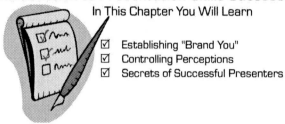

- ☑ Establishing "Brand You"
- ☑ Controlling Perceptions
- ☑ Secrets of Successful Presenters

"All the world is a stage."
William Shakespeare (1564 - 1616)

Welcome to your first step toward enhanced presentation skill success! You've worked hard and have overcome a variety of obstacles to be where you are today. Now you must focus on your presentation of self to soar to the next level.

In today's competitive world, your professional and social success depends on your ability to: present your ideas to your colleagues, make more effective client presentations on the job, feel more confident in social situations, and handle media opportunities with panache.

Celebrating "Brand You"

Business guru Tom Peters first came up with the concept "Brand You" a few years back, drawing attention to the fact that we, as business professionals, are "a brand" in the same way as a bar of Ivory soap.

Consciously or unconsciously, we package ourselves with the clothing we wish to wear, the way we project ourselves in business situations, and the manner in which we conduct ourselves in client meetings.

Savvy marketers know that the key to a successful product is strong brand identity. Soap is a familiar product, but as we stand in the supermarket aisle and look at the dozens of soaps available, our criteria in choosing a product is no longer about simply getting clean. We are looking for a familiar brand -- a trusted source -- and one with which we have a strong emotional connection.

As business professionals in a competitive market, clients will choose us in a similar way. The products and services we offer may be similar to our competitors, but people will engage us on the basis of our personal brand.

Improve Presentation Skills and Strengthen Your Brand

You subconsciously telegraph your brand in every interaction, no matter how brief or nonverbal. As you enter the elevator in a busy office building, everyone sharing the space with you is observing you, whether they are aware of it or not.

Behavior scientists have identified the fact that when individuals interact with others, each is silently and subconsciously making hundreds of different observations *per second*. Since this communication is nonverbal and happens in milliseconds, we are consciously unaware we are communicating at this level. It's valuable to note that without even speaking, we have been judged on our personality, our ability to inspire trust, and our intelligence.

Whether you are searching for business or personal success, the journey begins with enhanced presentation skills. This book is about improving your presentation skills when you present to colleagues, clients, and articulate your ideas in a public forum.

Presentation skills are not difficult to learn. In the course of our work together, we will cover the "basics" of everything you need to give effective client presentations and public talks.

These basics include:

- ☑ Secrets of developing an informative, entertaining talk;
- ☑ Methods of instantly engaging the audience;
- ☑ Radiating positive energy through eye contact;
- ☑ Increasing interest and energy with gestures;
- ☑ Why connecting with the audience is the most important element in your talk;
- ☑ Why you MUST learn to start with your "close" in mind — — and more!

Enhance Confidence

You will also learn easy ways to develop and bolster confidence in every aspect of your daily life, specifically the times when you are actively presenting and all eyes are upon you. Dazzling your audience when you are on the podium is only half the battle. The objective of this book is to help you achieve the kind of awareness that inspires true positive and lasting change.

On a practical level, this book outlines tips, tools, and techniques to prepare and deliver more effective client and/or sales presentations, as well as how to give more confident public talks. This book will help you unveil your unrecognized talent to shape a more successful image.

Be Perceived as you Wish Others to Perceive You

Most people don't think about the image they project on a conscious level. In reality, we are "always on display," but few realize it until we are "officially" under the spotlight and about to deliver a spoken message. Yet any time we appear in public, even when we silently stand in line at the grocery store, we are nonverbally revealing a dictionary's worth of information about ourselves.

The question is: are people receiving the "right message?"

Are you being perceived by others as you want them to perceive you?

Should you present yourself effectively in every situation, not just when you are "aware" of being in the public eye? Best selling brands achieve celebrity status because they are consistently delivering a well packaged, uniform and reliable message. A bar of fresh smelling *Irish Spring* soap with its energetic green wrapping does not change its colors when the store is closed and it assumes no one is watching.

Shakespeare made the line famous, but the world's greatest thinkers have treated the world as their stage for centuries.

If Archibald Leach Can Do It, So Can You!

Almost a century ago, Archibald Leach grew up an unhappy boy in a bleak English town, depressed by the mental instability of his institutionalized mother and a yearning for a better life.

On the streets of London, Archibald became entranced by the sophisticated, urbane, well dressed men who cut a dashing figure. He joined a theater troop in Manhattan, and began to mimic the dashing figures he admired as a young boy.

Once Archibald Leach changed his name, he quickly became that icon of elegance we recognize as the movie star Cary Grant.

Cary Grant's Success Secret

Famed psychhologist Carl Jung believed that our subconscious mind is a tool we can access and utilize in order to elevate from our present circumstances to achieve success in any area we wish.

Cary Grant saw a clear, direct path from his circumstances to stardom. He knew that to succeed, he had to believe that success was possible. In the same way, you must believe that you have within you the power to be an effective, persuasive presenter and speaker.

Grant had a vision, and a mission, and achieved his goals. So can you!

Ready to move forward and make your mark? Let's go!

Summary:

☑   Brand yourself with your values;

☑   Project yourself as a "total package;"

☑   Confidence occurs from the inside out;

☑   You have the power to telegraph a successful image.

Assignments:

1. Purchase a notebook and carry it everywhere to record observations you make of yourself and others. Train yourself to become "aware" of the messages others telegraph. Do they accomplish this with their clothes? Their manner? Walk? Posture?

2. **Create three lists.** One list should be made up of the qualities you appreciate most in yourself. Another list should contain qualities you admire in others and wish to attain for yourself. The third list should contain qualities you consider detrimental to your future progress.

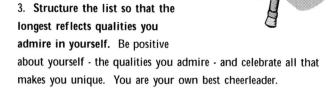

3. **Structure the list so that the longest reflects qualities you admire in yourself.** Be positive about yourself - the qualities you admire - and celebrate all that makes you unique. You are your own best cheerleader.

Chapter 2
Crafting a Dynamic First Impression

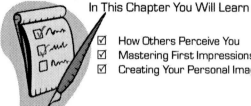

In This Chapter You Will Learn

☑ How Others Perceive You
☑ Mastering First Impressions
☑ Creating Your Personal Image

"Opportunity is missed by most people because it is dressed in overalls and looks like work."

Thomas A. Edison (1847 - 1931)

In today's fast paced business world, the image we convey to others is a reflection of our employer, our personal standards, and ourselves. Potential clients and business prospects must make split second decisions, often based on nothing more than how we are dressed, a quick handshake, and the manner in which we conduct ourselves.

As we venture into the exiting, high stakes game of crafting persuasive presentations and effective public talks, it's important to realize that first impressions have the power to make or break your career.

We have been told this since childhood, but it is important to firmly establish how important making the right first impression really is.

As Thomas Edison noted nearly a century ago, many are quick to dismiss very qualified people because they don't reflect "quality" within in their appearance.

Example: Shopping for a new house.

As you visit homes, your eyes and all your senses are on high alert. You take in the neighborhood, the cars of your potential neighbors, and visualize yourself driving up the driveway as if this was really your home.

You probably "felt" a certain way as you visualized the drive up, either "pride" or dissatisfaction with some aspect of the house or neighborhood.

Then, there was the house itself. Because it would be an important purchase, you probably inspected every aspect of it, at the same time clearly visualizing yourself living there.

When you enter a setting in which you could potentially be conducting business, even if the situation is social or casual, you are being judged in the same manner as the house. People meeting you for the first time will be visualizing what it would be like to work with you.

Just as you "tried the house on for size," potential clients and peers are looking at you in different ways to determine if you are suitable for a longterm relationship. They are quickly assessing if they can take pride in the relationship, your value quotient and long term pay off.

Controlling Image in a Presentation Setting

When you give a client presentation or a public talk, the pressure is kicked up several notches. Let's talk about a presentation first, since the situation is business and potential millions rest on your image and delivery.

How are you being perceived?

Before you answer, consider how harshly you may have judged others.

Attire is as Important as your Presentation

As busy, ambitious people prepare for a presentation, attire is often the last thing that comes to mind.   We all respect the time of our participants and want to deliver value to them. In the process we often exhaust ourselves creating groundbreaking content and dart out in our rumpled suits and worn-down heels in a rush to deliver that quality content.

But beware! All of your hard earned efforts will be for nothing unless your "visual persona" (i.e. your clothes, grooming, and demeanor) equals and/or virtually exceeds the quality of the material you are presenting.

For those of us who pride ourselves on our content, this is a very bitter pill to swallow. Why should our years of exhaustive education, hours of backbreaking research, and attention to the finest detail of our presentation have anything to do with an attribute so random and superficial as appearance?

Answering this question would require another book, but the short answer is that as human beings, we are "pre-wired" to take appearance into account in every area of our lives. A restaurant that slopped food on a plate would have few customers. The same is true of a restaurant that served great food, but the restaurant itself was filthy and unfinished.

In any presentation situation, the audience looks to our appearance first, then our manner of delivery, and finally, the content itself.

Are You a Supporting Character or the Headliner?

Is your suit freshly pressed? Your shoes shined? Your tie firmly knotted or your scarf on straight?

Have you ever seen a "buddy movie?" How can you tell the leading man or woman from their best friend?

Usually, the leading character is exceptionally well groomed. The friend is a bit more sloppy and casual. You've probably seen the film *When Harry Met Sally*. Both "stars" were attractive and clearly the feature players. Their best friends were quirky yet clearly second string. Pygmalion films such as *Pretty Woman* and *Working Girl* showed how successful the lead characters have become through visual cues. In both films, the characters played by Julia Roberts and Melanie Griffith had best friends who were cute but unsophisticated. By the end of the films, both Julia and Melanie had grown glamorous, sophisticated, gradually illustrated by physically contrasting them to their old friends.

Think about who you are, and your professional "role." If you were a Hollywood costume designer, how would you dress yourself?

Chances are, you haven't thought about the observations others make of us, as we make of characters on the silver screen or television. As you dress for your presentation, keep this analogy in mind.

Your Visual Appearance is Your Resume

Lawyers often spend hundreds of thousands of dollars engaging behavior scientists to "read" the clothing and grooming of jurors. These scientists have discovered that each moment, individuals are subconsciously taking note of up to a hundred visual signals we subconsciously send out through our mannerisms, our facial expressions, and our clothes.

These signals include often-overlooked details of dress and grooming. So, while your audience may not make any remarks about your appearance, and may not even "think" about your appearance on a conscious level, subconsciously they are noting every detail, including the fit, length and tailoring of your suit, its color, the choice of accessories, your hair (too long, too short, clean, greasy), your nails (bitten, manicured), and other smaller, but intensely revealing details such as the pen you use, the briefcase you carry, even noting if your shoes are shined.

In other words, the audience is looking at you before your talk and using the choices you've made about your appearance to answer a single question: *is this person worth listening to?* Dressing well will ensure this question is answered in the affirmative.

Matching Audience Expectations

When we enter a place of worship, we automatically expect that our spiritual leader will look the part. Imagine how surprising it would be for an individual we consider our spiritual advisor to appear in a torn or even spotted shirt. Here we are, anticipating someone who can lead us to salvation, and he can't even get the coffee stain off his shirt.

When we present, our audience has similar expectations of us. Because *the audience* has come to see *us*, in their mind they already consider us the ultimate expert on the subject and to be representative of that authority.

This is why it is absolutely crucial to defer to their expectations of what an expert looks like while maintaining the image we have of an expert in our minds.

This is a principle of the subconscious mind: "act as if" and it shall be so.

Posture and Bearing

Clothing is important. It's the most striking and obvious of all visual clues. Yet once we are done analyzing someone's clothing the next thing that captures our interest is their bearing. Do they hold themselves erect? Or are they hunched over, as if carrying a weight?

Susan, a portfolio manager, had ambitions for success. She dressed neatly and well, but walked with her shoulders lowered and slumped forward, which telegraphed lethargy on a subconscious level..

Once Susan was made aware of her posture, she corrected it and began to examine more seriously the messages she was subconsciously projecting to others.

Smile Power

A smile is the most powerful weapon in your arsenal for turning prospects into clients, and persuading others to your point of view. A smile telegraphs a wide array of positive positive messages, and has been clinically shown to make us actually feel better, since engaging the facial muscles in this way releases "feel good" endorphins.

When we smile, we are also conveying a subconscious "I'm okay, you're okay" attitude to the other party that lifts the energy of the entire room.

Many people would like to smile, but feel inhibited because of poor dental care. Good dental care is important, but a warm, welcoming smile enlivens your face and pumps up the energy in the room. Many people need to "train" themselves to smile. Surprisingly, it's not as easy as you think. Smiling is work, as any beauty contestant will testify.

We automatically smile when we see something amusing, but the kind of smiling successful people do is very much a self-directed effort. One must literally "put a smile" on her face. Try it now, you will see what I mean. Don't you feel a difference in your facial muscles?

Practice and soon smiling will become an automatic gesture. Begin by simply smiling at everyone. If you're usually a non-smiling person and are engaging in this practice for the first time, it will amuse and enlighten you to keep a notebook about the effect your smile has on others. You will quickly see that it elevates others and pre-disposes them to be more open towards you. Putting a smile in any interaction lightens your own mood.

Beware of Distracting Mannerisms

Recently, I saw an award winning commercial featuring a beautiful woman and a man who wanted to get to know her better. To test his devotion, she dropped one item after another from the top of a building and watched as he performed a series of death defying moves to retrieve each item.

Finally, she removed her teeth, dropped them from the building, and smiled toothlessly at him.

The gentleman's shock was the punch line of the commercial, surprising him as well as the audience. In the same way, no matter how well groomed and freshly pressed you are, a distracting mannerism can ruin the image you went to so much trouble to project.

What can this be?

Any number of distracting habits, hair twirling, coin jingling, cuticle pulling, and pen clicking chief among them. As distracting as these mannerisms can be in casual conversation, they can be devastating to a presentation or public talk.

The best defense is awareness. Train yourself to watch for these behaviors in your daily life. Videotape practice is your best friend, alerting you to potentially distracting behavior and reinforcing behavior that works. If videotape is not an option, ask a friend to watch your rehearsal and note if you engage in distracting behavior. If so, work to modify them.

The Snapshot and Camera Pan

The Snapshot and Camera Pan is a technique I created to help clients gain awareness of potentially distracting behavior. It can help you in three key ways. First, it quickly forces you to see yourself as others are really seeing you. Second, it creates the awareness that you are actually being seen, and gives you a perspective on how you are being observed. Third, the image is so visual you make the connection between your behaviors and their effect on others immediately.

What you do in both the snapshot and camera pan is imagine that you are the star on a TV reality show, and cameras are following you around twenty-four hours a day. You might even consider keeping a notebook to monitor your progress.

If you find the behavior difficult to break, replace the "footage" of the distracting behavior with that image of yourself the way you would like to be seen and regarded by others.

Remember, too, that it's impossible to "change" behavior unless you replace it. Identify another behavior with an advantageous benefit to you once you make the change.

For example, many speakers have developed the annoying habit of using "helping words" such as "uh" and "you know" into their presentations. It's said that nature abhors silence, and instinct motivates us to insert a sound when we are searching for something to say.

Simply telling yourself not to use these words is ineffective. Instead, *visualize* yourself replacing these words with a simple pause. As you will soon realize, a pause has real power. And by replacing one behavior with a more positive behavior (as opposed to simply telling yourself "not to grasp at words") you are being actively constructive.

Handshake Magic

The handshake extends from the days when men would shake to show they were unarmed. Today, the gesture suggests all parties are on an equal footing. It works on a subconscious level as it involves touching another individual and in its most ephemeral form is meant to telegraph trustworthiness.

Recall the advertisement from Allstate Insurance. It consists of two cupped, open palms with the headline: You are in good hands with Allstate.

Imagine you are buying insurance because you support a spouse and two young children, have just bought a nice house, and want your family to continue to live comfortably should something happen to you.

You really love your family, and you really MUST trust your insurance agent since the plan they devise for you must care for your family. You are literally putting yourself in your insurance agent's hands.

Now, imagine two agents. The first gives you a weak, damp, limp handshake. How much would you trust him? The second agent offers a firm, secure handshake clearly positioning himself as the trustworthy source.

Based on the handshake alone, whom would you select to be your agent?

You don't need to be a bone crusher to deliver an effective handshake. What you do need to realize is that subconsciously

your handshake is one of the strongest success tools you have in business. You can give it more power by looking in the person's eyes, and saying their name, as you pump hands.

Your handshake is somewhat like your signature, hard to change. But it can always be improved. Looking into the eyes of the other party and saying his name is a good place to start.

More on Names

Names have power. Names personalize us as human beings sharing space on this planet. The power of a name starts when we're small children, eager to get a "personalized" plate for our bicycle and continues to adulthood when special email programs use our name in the slug line of their email message.

I'd just like to note that executives routinely toss letters after a cursory glance, seeing their name is misspelled.

We are impressed when others remember our names, especially if we can't remember theirs or have met them only once.

But how can *you* remember the names of others?

Entire books are devoted to this subject, but the short answer is to focus as you hear the name. Imagine the name written on the forehead of the person you are talking to. Then, say it again. If appropriate, you can say "did I pronounce that right?" or "is it spelled this way?" These are all techniques that can help you remember names.

At the same time, take pity on others and always try to offer your own name as you meet. If someone familiar comes toward you, but you forget his or her name, extend a hand and warm smile and say, "Hi" -- being sure to give your full name.

Establishing an Image

The image we project is a combination of several factors. If someone is meeting us for the first time, much of the impression she receives is established through our physical appearance -- specificially the clothes we choose to wear and our personal accessories.

If the individual meeting us has "heard about us" from others, much of her image is formed from what she heard. If she has visited our web site, or seen our business stationery, she may form an impression of us based on the quality of the above-stated materials.

As stated before, quality counts in clothes as well as business accessories. My stationery is printed on unusually thick white paper (70 pound) with a subtle weave. The Deg.com logo is blue, and the designer arranged my contact information in an innovative way that borders on 'edgy.'

I tried to make my web site, http://www.deg.com, as similar to the design logo as possible. Blue was chosen specifically as the primary color because historically it conveys a sense of being trustworthy. When I speak, I usually try to wear a blue suit for the same reason.

Dress For the Future

How you dress depends on your industry, but a good rule of thumb is to dress for how you want to be seen in the future. Clothing sends a powerful message. A young attorney should dress as well as the partners, positioning herself from the start as "partnership material."

Dressing Well Can Save You Money!

Dressing well is an art that many Europeans have mastered, but which many Americans have yet to learn as a result of our mass-produced, "quantity over quality culture." Many Americans shop "to lift their spirits" and as a consequence, squander money on clothes which will not improve their image over the long run.

By contrast, Europeans are raised from birth to consider clothing a reflection of their inner selves. They are eager to dress as well as they can afford. Europeans usually buy quality merchandise in "basic colors," have it custom tailored, and become experts at changing the look entirely with accessories (shirts, blouses, scarves, ties). They might spend a bit more money initially on a suit or pair of shoes, but will save in the long term by avoiding trendy fashion items that do not underscore their core image.

Dressing 101

Everyone's situation is unique, but overall, men and women often face separate issues when it comes to dressing well.

Both sexes should be conscious of clothes that provide a firmly defined silhouette. This is particularly important when appearing on television interviews, but a firmly defined silhouette also gives you additional credibility in your daily business life.

The business-savvy silhouette can be identified by sharp, clean lines. Suit jackets are buttoned (psychologically also conveying the sense that you are literally "all together"), hair is neat, and the silhouette projects a sense of being ready for action.

The key element to perfecting this look is ensuring that the shoulders of your suit fit well. A personal preference is for slightly padded shoulders (both men and women) as it gives the wearer a more formidable presence. When people see you in the office, at the podium or in front of the boardroom, the silhouette savvy individual presents a commanding look of power and authority.

As discussed, when you project power and authority, people listen more carefully to what you have to say.

Tips for Men

Men frequently make the career-limiting mistake of thinking they can wear a suit "one more time" before having it pressed. They neglect to button their jacket when they are speaking while standing, their tie is sometimes stained, and their shoes can use a shine or repair.

Loose and missing buttons are another aspect of dress that men neglect to see the importance of. Most cleaners check for missing buttons and will certainly replace them on request. Make certain to request extra buttons if you buy an elegant blazer or other sports jacket with distinctive gold, silver, or signature buttons.

It's best to button your suit or sports jacket in a formal, and even, casual presentation. The reason? Psychologically, you look "more together." If you practice giving the same presentation on video with your jacket open and closed, you will see the difference.

Pants look best when they are fresh from the cleaners and have that sharp crease. Once again, the extra attention to this detail psychologically reinforces that you and your ideas are sharp. Shoes are of special importance, and should be new-looking, shined, and in good repair. Details count.

Hair length for men is a personal preference, but make certain hair is clean and styled so that it smoothly is pulled back from your face, even if you are in an industry where longer hair is common. Again, this reflects on the psychological concept of people perceiving "visual order" reflecting mental order and clarity.

Tips for Women

Because women have more flexibility in their wardrobe, they need to make sure the message they send with their clothing is correct.

It's a good idea to stick with the silhouette idea as mentioned above, as it enhances credibility. The silhouette rule as applied to women suggests that you should cut down on "frills" and anything that flows (i.e. a trailing scarf) rather than being pinned down (a scarf tucked into your shirt or firmly pinned around your neck). A free floating scarf is not only distracting, but it lessens the power of a strong, vertical silhouette.

Skirt Length

Women often need to reconsider wearing a short skirt or low necked suit in a business setting, as it can send the wrong message.

Avoid a short skirt if you are a panelist sitting on a raised dais. You may be asked to sit directly in front of the audience without a table between you. A short skirt may soon have the audience chanting "I see London, I see France ..."

Cindi, a client, revealed that written feedback on every single evaluation form after a talk praised her presentation, but suggested she avoid the low necked suit because it was so distracting they couldn't concentrate on her content" and "it detracted from her expertise."

Avoid Potential Blunders by Planning in Advance

Do you plan out your wardrobe for presentations or even meetings in advance? You should. Leaving wardrobe to the last minute can create these easily avoidable blunders:

- ☑ The pants or skirt of the suit do not match the jacket;
- ☑ The suit is stained;
- ☑ The suit (or shirt) is not pressed;
- ☑ The suit is full of lint and you forgot your lint brush;
- ☑ The tie or scarf is stained or does not match;
- ☑ You are wearing a "different" shoe on each foot;
- ☑ Your pantyhose has a run or your socks don't match;
- ☑ There is a small tear in your suit;
   or your suit no longer fits!

So take a few minutes, try everything on, and put everything in one place so you will be ready to jump into it (like a fireman) before your presentation. Comfort is also key. Stand up. Sit down. Lean over in front of a mirror. Ladies, sit down in front of a mirror, especially if your skirt is on the shorter side.

Other Grooming Tips

Grooming goes hand in hand with the fit and freshly pressed look of your clothes. Men might need to get into the habit of carrying a razor with them if they are presenting later in the day. Women should completely reapply makeup if several hours have elapsed before your talk.

For tips on "dressing for success," one would do well to see images in fashion magazines such as *GQ* or *Esquire* for men, or *Vogue* for women. In addition, see what newsmakers wear in *Time* and *Newsweek*.

A good way to get free fashion help is by asking polite, open ended questions of top sales people. This is best accomplished by dressing up (as if for a business meeting) and visiting one of the better department stores in your city. Seek a clerk who dresses well, moves with efficiency, and radiates a sense of quality.

Approach the clerk, explain you are a presenter and are looking for a conservative suit that accentuates your expertise, and see what he comes up with.

If you can't afford the suit, before you take it off make note of why it looks so good on you. Listen to the words the sales professional uses as he points out how well the shoulders fit, etc. Try to understand the terminology and what makes a suit "look good."

Then, shop around and try to find a suit with these qualities elsewhere, at a lower price. But, if you can't match it, go back and buy the expensive suit. You will be happy you did and it will pay off in the long run in terms of enhanced  confidence and lead to attracting more business.

Accessories are Important

Many women swear by a *classic* designer bag and shoes. If a scarf fits your personal style, you might want to make this accessory your signature. Men do well with classic, quality ties, cuff links, and of course, the almighty pen.

At his New York restaurant, chef Alain Ducasse literally made headlines by offering patrons their choice of designer pen with which to sign the very expensive check.

A quality pen not only looks good in the pocket while the presenter speaks, but is fills its intended purpose when it's your turn to look impressive while taking notes.

Creating an Image Collage

Image is central to your self-development. You may find it advantageous to get professional help from an image consultant, or by going to a quality store and finding a sales professional whose style you admire.

But chances are that you do have a sense of your own personal style. To bring it to the surface, consider the image collage.

In the course of helping people determine their style during corporate retreats, I use an exercise I call a "personal image collage."

In this scenario, you will be accessing the image you have of your "higher self" — the personification of the "ideal you."

Begin the exercise by gathering up several publications. With scissors in hand, cut out images of models wearing clothes that reflect the quality image you aspire to. Paste these images onto cardboard and soon you will have a vibrant collage that reflects your new image.

If you still feel you need to see a professional consultant after this exercise, do so, but bring the image collage so you are not starting from scratch.

Summary:

☑   Your atttire sets the tone for your presentation;

☑   Dress in conformance with audience expectations;

☑   Smile to radiate positive energy;

☑   See yourself as if on camera;

☑   Solid handshakes are crucial;

☑   Invest in quality business cards, stationery, etc.

☑   Buy classic suits of quality materials.

Assignments:

1. Begin to observe others. What does their clothing and grooming telegraph about them?

2. Are you stuck in a rut? Changing your image can have a huge impact on how you see yourself, and how others see you.

3. Create an image collage to see yourself as wish to be perceived.

Chapter 3
Understanding Communication Styles

In This Chapter You Will Learn

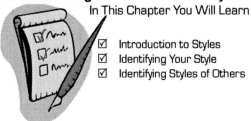

- ☑ Introduction to Styles
- ☑ Identifying Your Style
- ☑ Identifying Styles of Others

"They always say time changes things, but you actually have to change them yourself."

Andy Warhol (1928 - 1987)

Just as you have an image that visibly telegraphs your personality, your communication style colors your interactions with others.

Your personal communication style is the way you customarily act in specific situations, and when dealing with specific types of people. Your style is a curious mix of genetic coding, your natural temperament, and the way you successfully typecast and maneuvered successfully around others as a child.

Types of Personal Communication Styles

Are you a Mover? An Energizer? An Analyzer? Or an Agreer? These are names I personally use to describe the four basic communication/personality types. Some communication skills trainers use elements of the earth, and others use shapes or colors to describe communication styles. But I find the above words aptly summarize the key characteristics of each type.

Human beings have been typecasting people in tight little niches since the dawn of civilization. Originally, ancient cultures named nine distinct personality types and arranged them on a wheel known as the enneagram. Then the ancient Greek philosopher Hippocrates whittled these nine types into four, which he called "humours."

Famed psychoanalyst, Carl Jung, renamed the "humours" into four types identified as Sensing, Thinking, Intuitive, and Feeling. And finally, William Marston (who paved the way for the modern lie detector test) renamed Jung's types as Dominance, Influence, Steadiness, and Compliance and created the DISC anagram used in many sales training classes today.

Ancient Wisdom and Your Presentation

What does this ancient theory have to do with your upcoming presentation?

As educated adults, we know stereotyping is wrong. Yet in our time-crunched world we need to get a sense of who we are dealing with as quickly as possible to achieve success.

The Ideal Communicator

The ideal communicator is not a single type. Like the perfect multi-vitamin, an effective communicator is a well-balanced blend of all four types. By understanding and being able to communicate using the very best characteristics of the Mover, the Energizer, the Analyzer, and the Agreer, you have a complete toolbox at your fingertips.

With this toolbox, you can conduct yourself in an exemplary fashion where your best qualities wow clients over, and you have the intelligence to edit yourself and avoid potential snags.

Prospects and clients will be amazed at the way you seem to "understand them" and quickly make use of your services. All this, because you've taken the time to understand the four distinct types of human behavior.

Below are the characteristics of these styles in detail.

ANALYZER
- Fact-Oriented
- Bullet-Point Oriented
- Dilligent

MOVER

- Efficient
- Systematic
- Decisive

AGREER

- Supportive
- Motivating
- Team Player

ENERGIZER

- Dramatic
- Dependable
- Captivating

Can you identify one style that seems to characterize you best?

Let's look at a classic film to bring the definitions home. In the film *Gone with the Wind*, Scarlett O'Hara is the "Energizer." Gentle Melanie Hamilton would be the "Agreer." Rhett Butler a "Mover" and Ashley Wilkes the "Analyzer."

Where do you fit in? In truth, most people are a blend of two personality/communication styles, not just one.

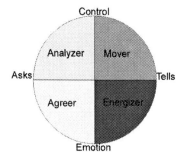

Common Communication Style Pairing

Most people will find that they are either an Analyzer/Agreer blend or an Mover/Energizer blend. In anticipation of the exercise to come position the types on a grid, like so.

Logic & Control Vs. Emotions

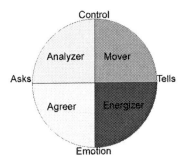

Consider the fact that even though Analyzers and Movers are "on the same side", both can be characterized as operating from **logic and control** rather than emotion. The primary difference between their systematic, logical methodology is that the Analyzer is prone to "ask" whereas the Mover simply "tells."

The Agreer and the Energizer both operate from emotion and sentiment. The difference here is also that the Agreer is prone to "ask" whereas the Energizer simply "tells."

Styles In Action

In the film *Wall Street*, Michael Douglas played a character who was controlling, demanding, and dictatorial, the classic Mover/Energizer personality with "Mover" being the dominant type. The mover is confident, self-reliant, plays to win, and feels the end justifies the means.

You know the type. Can you imagine this person "asking" for anything? They don't ask permission, they don't wait for "go," they march forward.

So, you might ask, what's wrong with that?

On the movie screen, these characters are fun to watch. We might even admire them, but as presenters, they need to tone down to exude a more likable image.

Toning Down and Building Up

In order for communication styles to tone themselves down or build themselves up, draw a line towards their diagonal opposite and seek to incorporate some of those dynamics into their style.

Let's use the "Mover" type represented by Michael Douglas in the film *Wall Street.* If he would look to his diagonal opposite, which is the "Agreer," and incorporate the qualities of the Agreer, he would effectively tone down some of the overbearance and be closer to the ideal presenter in representing the best of all four qualities.

The Agreer, a team player in the fullest sense of the word, is supportive, emotionally giving, and respectful of everyone's feelings. The Agreer is also a good listener, an action the self-centered Mover needs to do more of.

Another film example is *Pretty Woman,* where Julia Roberts played an Energizer. She came across as stimulating, enthusiastic, and quickly began to energize, motivate and inspire everyone around her. Julia's character enabled her love interest, played by Richard Gere, to accept making a commitment, and motivated her prostitute friend to go back to beauty school.

But what qualities would she need to "balance" her life, let alone give a more effective presentation?

As an Energizer she should look diagonally across to her opposite, the Analyzer: orderly, serious rather than superficial, and solid. As presenters, Analyzers are certain to back up their material with facts, statistics, and verifiable data.

Analyzers should also look diagonally across to their opposite, the Energizer, by condensing some of the facts and adding an anecdote or colorful story in true Energizer style.

Agreers need to add more "bite" to their presentations. They should look diagonally across to the Mover and act with verve from a position of strength and firm opinion.

Identifying the Style of Others

Identifying the style of others is more important in a one-on-one situation than a group dynamic or public talk. When in an one-one-one scenario, how do you identify someone's style quickly?

Movers and Energizers are traditionally more assertive than fifty percent of the population, so this is a good tip-off. Consider also how they talk and move. These types move quickly, with rapid, sure actions. They speak more than they listen, and their minds seem to work at a very high speed.

By contrast, Agreers are slow to respond as first wait until they are certain you will find their response agreeable. They will also speak in emotional terms, such as using the word "feel" instead of "think."

Analyzers are identified by their detail-oriented nature. They rarely voice their opinion until they've had time to see, and weigh, the facts of the matter.

Use Special Words For Specific Types

Specific words and phrases are music to the ears of each type. The correct selection of terminology telegraphs that you two are on the same wavelength and the same page.

For example, Movers like bold action words and phrases. They think in bullet points and love it when you list items to be addressed, use catch phrases like "let's cut to the chase" and "here's the bottom line."

Energizers respond to ideas. They are of the "build a field and they will come" mindset. They feed off your energy, so often, it's enough to inspire them and they will sell themselves on your idea. Use of vivid language creates a vivid mind picture -- the Energizer will take and run away with. Words like "picture this" and "imagine if" are highly effective to this type.

The thing to remember when dealing with the Agreer personality is that you must never rush them. They work from gut instinct, and perhaps more than the other styles need to really trust you before they can even hear what you are saying. So prepare to spend some time, ask about their aunt and their cat, and make small talk *before* getting down to business. Nodding in agreement, using the actual word "agree" along with emotional words like "feel" will lead an Agreer to your desired destination.

When you meet with an Analyzer, don't even approach them unless you are armed to the teeth with facts, figures, statistics, pie charts, and more to support your position. Like Sgt. Friday on the old TV series *Dragnet,* "just the facts, please."

Summary:

☑   Identifying your communication style helps you identify the style of others;

☑   Strive to incorporate the positive styles of others in your presentations;

☑   The four styles includes the Analyzer (who supports with facts), the Agreer (who wants to keep peace) , the Mover (who enjoys rocking the boat), and the Energizer (who uses charm and manipulation to achieve their aims);

☑   Identifying the communication style of clients and modifying your presentation accordingly make them more receptive to you.

Assignments:

1. Identify your communication style. Given your past presentations, what styles and traits do you need to incorporate?

2. Identify the style of two of your clients. How can you adapt yourself to their style?

3. Consider a boss or colleague? How can understanding the various style types make you a more effective communicator?

Chapter 4
Preparing to Present

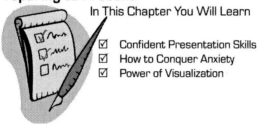

In This Chapter You Will Learn

☑ Confident Presentation Skills
☑ How to Conquer Anxiety
☑ Power of Visualization

"*If you tell the truth, you don't have to remember anything.*"
Mark Twain

Do you struggle to memorize a talk? Are you afraid that you will "freeze" and forget all or part of your presentation? Mastering presentation skills is not about "memorization." As Mark Twain so simply and eloquently explains, the best presentations come from the confidence of how well we know our subject – and how confident we are of ourselves.

Presenters are assumed to be experts on our topics. We are paid for our knowledge, yet why do experts who make six and seven figures a year suddenly lack confidence when they present? Why do many of these same experts fail to communicate their ideas clearly via the spoken word?

Each authority has their theories. To me, this a result of:

1. The presenter failing to differentiate the vast difference between written and oral communication, and assuming that success in written form equals success as a speaker;

2.   95% of the preparation time devoted to content organization and memorization, rather than techniques to make an emotional connection with the audience;

Confidence on the podium or selling floor is a direct result of three key elements.

1. Knowing your audience's need and reason for being there;
2. Slanting the talk to the specific audience, in advance;
3. Assuring the audience in every way you are there to give them value.

In the course of this chapter, you will discover the tools of delivering a confident presentation.

Benefits of Confident Presentation Skills

Speaking in public, whether for a small client presentation or a larger public talk, can enrich us in many ways.

Listed here are just a few of the benefits:
1. We deepen our authority as experts;
2. We promote our abilities;
3. We make key connections;
4. We gain a bit of notoriety from the media and our peers;
5. Public speaking brings new opportunities;
6. We deepen our foundation of knowledge;
7. We create an opportunity for more business;
8. We create broader marketing opportunities.

A confident presenter communicates ideas clearly. Presenters who lack confidence are often worried about their own personal performance in the eyes of their audience and lose track of the message. This shaky performance has roots on two levels, the conscious and the subconscious.

Many people assume that speaking to a group is similar to communicating on radio where one person speaks and the other listens until the situation is reversed.

Speaking in public is actually more of a party line. It is a two-way dialogue between the speaker and the members of the audience, even though the speaker is usually the one doing all the talking. The reason for this is the speaker must feed on the audience's enthusiasm and energy to communicate effectively.

The speaker must be focused and confident to monitor the audience's interest level. Is the material familiar to them? Are they "getting it?" Are there questions that need to be addressed before you move forward?

Establishing Confidence

You are confident and comfortable when you're on your own turf and in familiar settings. Unfamiliar environments often put us off guard.

One way to increase confidence and thus deliver a better presentation is to visit the location where you are to present before you begin, or at least arrive early enough to get a sense of the room and use visualization to see yourself giving an effective presentation.

As you stand in the room where you are to speak, imagine an enthusiastic audience. Liberace, the late entertainer, used to sneak into the Hollywood Bowl and play the piano, imagining thousands of adoring fans.

If entering the room before your presentation is impossible, you can still use visualization to see yourself giving an effective presentation. Vividly see the familiar faces you know will be there. Envision success.

You Control Perceptions!

You alone control the perception others make of you.

As I have mentioned and will expand on in later chapters, those to whom you present make their initial judgments on a nonverbal level. When you first open your mouth to speak, they are not hearing your words. They are forming an impression on a visual level, first determining if you are credible and that your words have value.

You are radiating your message nonverbally by projecting your sincerity and authority to speak on the topic. At this level, a charlatan would have more success "snowing over" a crowd than a well-credentialed speaker lacking confidence.

Why? Think about people who make their living by fraud and deception. They have learned to telegraph sincerity and authority on a deeply subconscious level.

The charlatan subconsciously radiates success, authority, mastery, etc., leading the crowd to their desired outcome, such as having them up on their feet with a standing ovation. Behold the art of snake charming at its best.

Conversely, the well-credentialed speaker lacking confidence in his/her ability to persuade a crowd (or even a small group during a client presentation) will receive no ovation, despite the inherent brilliance of their talk. The cracking voice, mumbled words, face firmly directed downward at their notes, will subconsciously signal to the audience that the speaker's tentative delivery represents a lack of faith in their subject.

So, how can we rev up our confidence level?

First, realize that a great presentation is more than "wishing" or "visualizing" success. A brilliant talk and hours of practice won't get you the glory you deserve unless you "feel" success as due reward for your hard work. If you are in the least bit apprehensive "if" your talk will be well received, you are leaving too much to chance. Visualizing success is the first step.

But remember. You have to reinforce visualization with the more physical aspect of success, such as good writing, practice, practice, and yet more practice.

Learned Behaviors

When you sit down to dinner, you usually don't have trouble aiming that fork full of pasta toward your mouth, do you? You don't have to consciously think about maneuvering the fork so it lands in the right place.

But when you were a baby, your parents spent months helping you train yourself to know where your mouth was located.

The same principle is involved when you drive a car. In driving school, you had to "think" to put your foot on the accelerator. Now, you get into your car, and often find yourself at your destination without remembering anything about the trip.

The above two examples represent learned behaviors that have become "habits" from years of practice. Given five minutes, you could think of hundreds of other learned behaviors that turned habitual over the years.

Visualization to SEE a Positive Outcome

Ask any athlete and he will tell you that visualizing success is part of his daily life. Before every race, he is already seeing himself clearly as he tears through the finish line.

Would just "visualizing it" be enough if he didn't practice?
No, of course not.

But the visualization of winning motivates him to practice since his focus is consistently on the goal.

You're a Better Presenter Than You Think You Are

It's true. *How do I know?*

Too many of us "shake off" compliments, flushing them out of our system before the complimentary statement is complete.

The #1 rule to understand is that you must create a bank of compliments in order to manifest self-confidence when you need it most.

Why?

Consider a car. Cars manufactured to look great and take you where you want to go, right? Why would you buy a car if it looked terrible and didn't run because it lacked fuel? When we present, we are very much like a car. We are expected to look good and take the audience to another level.

We will be believed by our audience only to the extent we believe ourselves. That full bank of compliments serves as the fuel resource to get you to that next level of confidence.

Those of us lucky enough to have encouraging parents who inculcated in us the power that we had the ability to be whatever we wanted to be are several steps ahead of those who didn't.

Realize that you have the power to "catch up" in a very short
period of time, but it you must make this a key priority.

I encourage you to start immediately, because the most valuable
gifts you can ever give are gifts you give to yourself.

Does this sound selfish? Self-serving?

Consider the flight attendant's safety instruction you hear
before each flight. She reminds us that if we are traveling with a
small child, we must first put the oxygen mask on ourselves, and
then the child. We need to make sure we're fully functioning
before we can attempt to help others.

Effective Presenters Create Positive Vibrations in the Room

Energy is contagious. The hallmark of an effective speaker is
an individual who radiates positive vibrations, which, in turn,
consciously or unconsciously ignites and motivates the creativity
of those around them. Just the other day, I found myself at my
local Chamber of Commerce networking event, where Vicki
Donlan, publisher of *Women's Business*, gave a talk on networking
that raised the positive vibrations in the room.

Was the talk different or unique from most other networking
talks?

No.

It was Donlan's energy, confidence, and colorful anecdotes
that created an almost visible energy flow. Anecdotes are great
ways to better connect with an audience, because it helps them
map your key points to their own experience.

Secret of Mastering Presentation Skills

Master presenters celebrate their most wonderful qualities and
positive beliefs about themselves, projecting them to what we can
conveniently call a "higher self."

Do as they do and visualize your own higher self, full of
wonderful qualities, and tap into its power as you present.

Always remember, your audience wants you to be fantastic.
They want and expect that "higher self" of yours to inspire *them*

to greatness.

Establishing Goals

Goals do turn into reality. History is filled with examples of people who literally dreamed the "impossible dream" and achieved overwhelming success against all odds. The "secret" of their success is that they worked on their goals with a laser-like focus.

Step One: Write It Down

Goals are free floating, random ideas until you write them down. Ancient Egyptians believed goal setting was sacred, even magical. The two primary Egyptian rules are:

1. Give a "Name" to what you desire and make the goal as specific as possible.

This is important. If you just want to "present better" — well, better than what? Better than you are now? Just a few degrees better, or do you wish to attain the skills of a true professional?

2. Give your desires written form.

This turns an "energy pulse" in your brain into the first step of manifestation.

To develop confidence when you present, it is necessary to make confidence a clearly outlined goal. For the goal to "register" with your subconscious mind, it must be written down.

Writing Your Goals

As you write your goals, make sure that you have a "completion date" when you expect the goal to be met.

You also will want to write a mission statement, written in the first person. For example, your mission statement might be: "In 21 days, I will actively work on increasing my level of confidence to the point where I will enjoy giving talks and can see that the talks are well enjoyed and understood by my audience."

Reinforce this mission statement with your own interior "audio" and "video." In other words, see yourself working on the steps outlined in this book, and then flash foward to a picture of yourself giving your presentation. Feel your new level of confidence. See the audience nod in response to your words of widsom. See their hands clap together as they leap to their feet and you hear a standing ovation and they tell you how great you were.

The Magic Trio: Affirmations, Visualization, Treasure Mapping

Confidence is developed from within and takes place in the subconscious mind. One of the quickest ways to tap into its power is through positive affirmations.

Positive Affirmations

Positive affirmations are building blocks to greater confidence and infuse our presentations with power. Using them freely and often reinforces your positive qualities and cancels out any negative thoughts or "worries" that may come your way.

The basic premise of an affirmation is to give reinforcing positive messages. The messages can be:

- ☑ Performed silently
- ☑ Spoken aloud
- ☑ Written down
- ☑ Ideally, a combination of all three.

The key is to develop a steady stream of silent positive affirmations running through your mind at all times.

How to Benefit From Your Positive Affirmations

1. Always phrase affirmations in the present tense (as if what you desire already exists);
2. Phrase affirmations in an enthusiastic way;

3. Short, direct affirmations are more easily remembered and are the most effective.

Shakti Gawain, author of the book *Creative Visualization*, recommends that you take an affirmation and write it ten to twenty times on a piece of paper using your name in the first, second, and third person.
For example:

☑ I, Paul Presenter, am a great presenter;
☑ Paul Presenter, your image is that of a great presenter;
☑ Eddie Entrepreneur just gave a great presentation yesterday.

Banish Mind-Yapping

What is mind yapping? It is allowing negativity to interfere with your success. People who achieve things in life refuse to let negativity stop them. Let's say a civil engineer, Alex, has a brilliant idea that save his company money and get him a promotion and a raise. He's fired up, ready to talk to his boss, when the mind-yapping thoughts come in like dark clouds on a sunny day. *What if the boss thinks it's a stupid idea?* Alex thinks. *What if the boss grabs the idea for himself and gets a promotion out of it. What if he hears the idea and gets jealous I'm smarter than he is and fires me? Oh, why bother anyway, nobody ever does anything new here, anyway.*

And so, Alex talks himself out of his idea.

Maybe you're thinking: *Not me! Why should I sabotage myself?*

Psychologists have considered several common reasons:

1. Success is a responsibility;
2. You want your life to drastically change, yet you're afraid of change at the same time;
3. Becoming a success will change the direction of your life forever, and you're not sure you want it changed;
4. Secretly, you fear you can't measure up;

Combat mind yapping with a one-two punch. First, recognize a negative thought for what it is: a mind-yap. Remove the negative thought by getting into the habit of immediately replacing it with two positive thoughts.

How to Tap into the Power of Your Subconscious Mind

Visualization is one of the most important tools you will learn in your life and in this book. Psychologist Carl Jung and others have identified a direct correlation between visualizing a goal or desire, and seeing it manifest in reality through the power of the subconscious mind.

The mind is a powerful tool that operates best on a visual plane. When you think of a vacation in the Caribbean, you see the palm trees and the blue water, you don't see the word.

In the same way, the mind regards all events equally. The mind/body response does not differentiate between past, present, future, or imagination. Each registers as an *image*. Conditioning your mind to see yourself as confident and positive is one of the fundamental components of this process to achieving excellence while making a presentation.

There are three fundamental elements for effective visualization.

Desire: You must clearly see the advantages and probability of becoming that confident speaker which now seems a distant dream.

Belief: You must believe that you have the strength, talent, and ability to attain your goal.

Acceptance: You must accept that confident speaking is possible.

Before I give a presentation, I make it a key point to visualize the presentation in my mind's eye as if watching a movie. In this case, you are the director of the movie -- so see it flow as positively as possible.

Some people "worry" too much to even visualize a great presentation. Still others are so nervous and apprehensive, they skip the preparation entirely, simply thinking they will "get through" it one way or another. As you can imagine, neglecting to practice and prepare results in a lukewarm reception, or worse.

The "worse" hits the speaker in different ways. Sometimes it's a flurry of bad evaluation forms. Other times, the speaker actually sees attendees leave the classroom. Speakers who are convinced of their potential just take it in stride, and realize there is no "cheating" -- they will have to put in the preparation time.

But others internalize the negative reception. They have a negative association in their mind, which must be broken and replaced by a new, positive link.

How you "break" this negative link is a matter of preference, and some degree of entertainment. Some like to imagine negativity as a deteriorating film, ultimately flying out of the projector in every direction. Others see it "crack" as in a mirror. Negativity can burst into flames. However you want to destroy it, the choice is yours.

Replace the old tape and its negative associations with a positive, brand new movie featuring yourself giving a successful talk.

Imagine this setting as completely as possible. Try to visit where you will be giving the presentation, or use past experiences in similar venues to put together an Oscar winning mind picture.

Visualize yourself performing well. See the details of what you will be wearing, down to your shoes. Imagine your PowerPoint slides (if you will be using them) as they exist now.

As you play the movie in your mind, notice everyone's heads nodding in agreement. Then, after the talk, hear a burst of excited applause.

You've arrived!

Acting "As If"

Working under the assumption you are a confident speaker is a surefire way of transforming your goal to reality. From this point forward, visualize yourself five to ten times a day speaking with confidence. Be certain to see the audience and note their positive reaction to you. Be in the moment!

Tips for Creative Visualization

1. See your visualization session as a "reward" instead of something you "have to do."

2. Give yourself an actual reward for your sessions, at least in the beginning, even if it's just a verbal compliment or affirmation to yourself.

3. Create a very clear mental image of how great you'll feel as you achieve each step of your goal.

Treasure Mapping

A treasure map is a collage that you create around how you want to be perceived by the audience. It is another tool to help your subconscious mind focus on the image you want to manifest for yourself as a presenter. Treasure maps draw power and energy to your transition as represented by the map.

The treasure map imprints itself on your whole brain, absorbing colors, shapes, and images. Your natural intuition will be heightened to the point that you will find yourself meeting extraordinary people who influence your life in a positive way. As if magnetically charged, you will draw more impact to your presentation with little effort.

Here are the materials you'll need to map:

1. Magazines to cut up
2. Poster board, any size and color
3. Glue stick, scissors

You can also use postcards, lightweight toys or souvenirs, and Internet images, especially if you can print out in color. When you're gathering materials, be sure to find an assortment, especially items containing images and headlines that suit your story.

Once you have all the materials at hand, begin by visualizing yourself about to present before a group of clients or an audience.

Visualize the audience looking at you with admiration and expectation. Then, turning to your magazines, flip through the pictures rapidly, snipping all images that reflect this visualization.

If you need words and phrases that you can't find in magazines, you can create and print them out from your computer. As always, choose the font size and type that's most inspiring to you.

Assemble the images and words in collage fashion, the way you might have when you were a child. I like to get brightly colored poster board that's roughly twice the size of copy paper. I work quickly as I paste the images in order to let my subconscious mind direct the process.

Once you have completed the map, it's important to place it where you can see it regularly. For example:

- ☑ Across from your desk;
- ☑ Directly on your computer screen as wallpaper (scan it in);
- ☑ Put it in the notebook that you have been carrying with you.

You can create as many Treasure Maps as you want. Realize they have power, and make sure you really want to manifest what you create.

Conquering Anxiety

Fear is a learned behavior. Humans are born "pre-wired" to make quick positive/negative associations between experiences that serve to guide us through our lives. Most of us will only have to touch a candle flame once as a child to avoid it forever. If we do something wrong and are punished, we form a link between the experience and the consequences.

As we get older, the pleasure/pain link becomes tied to psychological issues as well. Peer pressure and the desire to conform are strong in childhood and adulthood. Making a mistake, particularly one in public, is a cause for anxiety.

Delivering a presentation is scary for many people who give talks on rare occasions. Since the occasional talk is unfamiliar, we become anxious and associate anxiety to the event. After all, our peers are watching! What if we make fools of ourselves?

Fear sets in!

Consider that *Fear* is an Acronym for *False Evidence Appearing Real*

Fear is "not real." It is the result of a vivid, but imaginary, feeling of what *might* happen. Subconsciously, we may have been vividly envisioning our peers criticizing our talk. This is why it's important to program your subconscious mind so you **only** see a successful outcome. Just visualizing success will give you confidence you need to achieve your aim.

Many professional speakers reveal they feel "butterflies" the first few moments before their talk. Most say they use this adrenaline as a form of energy to drive their talk.

But this has no basis in reality, when it's very possible that your peers can be impressed by our talk. This gives us confidence, instead of fear.

What does this tell us?

That "we give ourselves anxiety," and that fear is an imaginary situation with no basis in reality.

We control how we respond to any situation, including speaking in public. We can either be fearful and have anxiety, or recognize fear for what it is and embrace confidence.

Confidence on the podium is a direct result of:

☑ **Knowing your audience.** What are their objectives in listening to your talk? What knowledge do they want to gain?

The closer you can hone in on what answers they seek, the more they will value and appreciate your talk.

☑ Appearance

Dress in the manor that will impress your audience and firmly establish you as the credible authority you are.

Every time you buy a new suit or other article of clothing, you are attempting to manipulate the impression you make on others. Appropriate attire for appropriate situations, will always draw a positive impression.

Yet as important as dress and grooming are to setting the tone of your presentation, how can you explain presenters who lack visual polish yet are magnetic? What was their secret? **Confidence** and **self-esteem** flying at their highest levels.

Are You Seeing the Picture As It Is "Really" Painted?

Many of us have developed the habit of looking at a situation from the worst possible angle, causing us to make projections that aren't in the least accurate.

Recently, I watched my friend, Julie, give a talk to colleagues about etiquette to an audience that presumably knew almost as much about the topic as she did herself. When she finished her presentation, she rushed up to me.

"That couple near you. They kept frowning during my talk. I must have disappointed them."

"No! You didn't hear them," I explained. They were telling one another how good you were!"

It's natural to feel "on the spot" when you're giving a presentation, but when you are delivering information in a confident, entertaining, and informative way, any "whispering" you might hear is praise.

Summary

☑   FEAR is an acronym for "false evidence appearing real;"

☑   Set the stage for audience appreciation via your image and mental attitude;

☑   Banish negative thinking with positive affirmations;

☑   You can control the perception others make of you;

☑   Write your goals for success.

Assignment:

1. Write down ten positive affirmations about your qualities as a presenter. Write in the present tense to emphasize and reinforce that your goals and objectives have already been achieved.

2. Create a Treasure Map for motivation and place it where you will see it regularly.

Chapter 5
Presentation Tips, Tools, & Techniques

In This Chapter You Will Learn

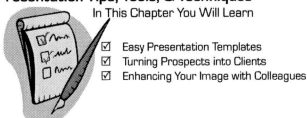

☑ Easy Presentation Templates
☑ Turning Prospects into Clients
☑ Enhancing Your Image with Colleagues

"Imagination is the beginning of creation. You imagine what you desire, you will what you imagine and at last you create what you will."
George Bernard Shaw (1856 - 1950)

Every day, in every way, you are selling yourself and your ideas. In today's competitive business environment, it's also important to reinforce your value to your peers and superiors in order to accelerate your career path, and stay employed.

The most effortless way to sparkle and shine is to implement simple, effective, time-tested techniques to raise yourself above the competition in every situation.

You accomplish this by establishing a template for presenting your ideas to clients and peers.

Gathering Information To Fill The Presentation Template

Consider the presentation template as a fill-in form that contains standard information and establishes a basic format. From the basic template you customize the content and focus it toward the target audience to outshine the competition.

For a generic presentation you will start with an introduction, progress to a statement of your main message supported by three key points (each of which are in turn supported by facts, statistics, and anecdotes), and summarize with a conclusion.

As you will soon discover, customization is the secret that differentiates your presentation template from the others.

Knowledge is Power

In the film *Groundhog's Day*, Bill Murray played a character who was turned down by the girl of his dreams time and again ... until he entered a magical realm in which he relived the same day over and over. This allowed him a second, third, and fourth chance to study the girl's likes and dislikes and mold himself into her ideal man.

Once Murray comes to know the hopes, fears, and desires of his love interest, he is perfectly positioned to win her heart.

As a presenter, the more you know about your audience, the more successful you will be. If you are speaking to a company or association, try to interview participants in advance or put together a pre-program survey. If you are speaking to a general audience, do some serious thinking about who would attend the ceremony, and the information they are most interested in.

Discover Hidden Desires

Let's face it. Each and every one of us is looking for a magical solution to our problems. Successful salespeople excel because they are experts at identifying what their target audience *really* wants. Next they craft their message using language that caters to their targets' needs.

Marketing executives at Jenny Craig (a popular diet program) accept that their customers' need is to lose weight. But weight is a relative term. What these clients really want is to be sexy, desirable, and have people look at them with admiration.

Jenny Craig executives cater to this need in the most visceral way possible, using enticing language that promises svelte bodies and visual word-pictures to show prospects how quick, fast, and easy their products will help customers attain the results they crave.

Research: Your Secret Cheat Sheet

Savvy presenters make it their business to know everything about their target market. They compile data and develop prototypes of potential clients, right down to how many children they have and bags of potato chips they consume each year.

Have you ever bought a book from Amazon.com? If so, you know that before you can escape, a flood of enticing titles will bombard you. Each title appeals to one of your interests, based on past buying history. The strategy works. Any time you can present a prospect with products or services tailor made to suit their needs, they are more likely to buy.

Find a Need and Fill It

Hollywood has a reputation for going too far when it comes to filling needs, and here's a true life story from the trenches. When I was starting out in Hollywood, I had a friend who worked for William Morris — let's call him J.

Like most guys in the mailroom, J. had a law degree — and was anxious to move up the ranks, Hollywood style, which meant finding a desk job as an assistant to a high-powered agent.

One day, J. decided he wasn't going to sit back and waste any more time. He was going to create the need that he would fill.

So while the agent was at lunch, J. zipped up to the agent's office and unscrewed a ball bearing from his chair. Then, J. lurked outside the office when the agent returned.

"What the #$%!" the agent screamed as the chair fell apart and he splattered on the floor.

"I'll fix it, sir!" said J, quickly moving in with — you guessed it — a ball bearing.

Impressed, the agent hired him as his assistant and now J. is head of one of the most successful agencies in Hollywood and a multimillionaire.

Playing Spy: Internet Sites That Win You Clients

Where and why do we "spy" on clients and companies when we know that no one likes to be spied upon? The Internet.

In today's sleek information age, you can get the lowdown on almost anyone or any company, for free. The Net is littered with sites giving financial and other information on top companies.

Try Hoovers.com, Marketwatch.com, CeoExpress.com, CnnFn.com and others you can find using a search engine such as google.com. Many of the sites are set-up to be "fee-based" but virtually all offer more than enough free information to get you the basic information you need.

What Information Should You Be Looking For?

A company willing to hear your presentation is concerned with only two issues:

☑ How can you help them achieve their long-term vision;

☑ How can you help them achieve short-term profitability.

Right now, while it is still fresh in your mind, think about the company you will soon present to. What do you feel is their long-term vision? And — market conditions being what they are — how can you help them be profitable for the next few years?

Think Like a CEO

Another thing to keep in mind is to think from the vantage point of a CEO. From this new point consider that their interest in you is not just what pension fund or widget you're trying to sell them, but *taking the load off their shoulders by showing them their own internal challenges* and how you've hand-selected the product or service that will *solve* that challenge. Create that need they didn't know.

Let your competitor make a sales pitch by rote, without a deep understanding of the client's needs. Position yourself as the professional whose mandate is to be a source of trust and value to the client. In this way, they will feel they are getting a bargain: their own "consultant" in addition to the purchase price of the product or service.

Personalize Your Presentation Through Questioning Skills

Internet research provides a strong foundation for learning the mission and vision of the prospect, but nothing can replace interviewing skills.

Popular stereotypes portray the average sales professional as a "talker." And yes, many sales people do have the gift of gab, and feel they are being "proactive" and "doing their job" when they speak. Listening is considered a passive behavior. But that's *only* if you don't know what you're listening for.

In the jargon of sales shorthand, what you're listening for is the client's pain. Remember, popular psychology tells us that people only buy when they are enticed by the prospect of pleasure or frightened by the prospect of pain. In a competitive market, customers will only buy from you if they perceive you to have the solution that addresses their *exact* need.

In his best selling book *How to Win Friends and Influence People*, Dale Carnegie warns against "over explaining" by using the anecdote of a salesman who scored a huge carpet account over dozens of other salesmen because he had laryngitis and the client ended up talking himself into the deal.

Talking, instead of listening, can be unwise for a two key reasons. First, you're making assumptions about the prospect's needs that may not be correct, and second, you are making it very easy for the prospect to cut you off and explain they're not interested in what you're selling.

Examples of Open Ended Questions

Open-ended questions are techniques to begin a balanced dialogue. They are broad in scope and designed specifically to learn more about the client and jump-start the conversation.

They motivate the prospect to share his/her thoughts, feelings, and concerns.

Below are some examples.

1. What do you see are the biggest challenges in your business?
2. What are your priorities for this project?
3. What qualities are you looking for in a new supplier?

Confirm What You Think You Are Hearing

Sometimes what you think you hear isn't necessarily what the client is saying. Whenever possible, confirm with a statement such as "If I understand you correctly, you're saying ..." or "As I hear it, you are suggesting ..."

Whether you are meeting with the client in person, or on the phone, show you are "actively listening" by injecting phrases that subconsciously encourage them to keep talking. Statements like "Tell me more!" and "I see" will usually do the trick.

What active listening does is subconsciously position you on the prospect's team. Using a lot of "we statements" suggests that you are tackling the challenge together.

If you are questioning the client in person, be certain to take notes! It's very flattering to the client to think that his words are taken seriously, and you will have concrete notes to use for your presentation. A nice psychological touch is using a quality writing instrument and smart looking leather notepad to jot down his valued words. Don't ever forget the image you are trying to project.

Personalizing The Presentation Template

As you customize the presentation template using information you gleaned from your prospect's open-ended questions and Internet research, be watchful for buzzwords your prospect may have reinforced in conversation. Echoing these words in your presentation is a powerful way to strengthen the bond you are developing.

In addition, refer back to your Internet research for buzzwords and/or key concerns the CEO may have mentioned in his mission statement or prior talks. The more you can relate what you have to sell to the company's mission or goal, the further along you will be towards the sale.

Look again at the notes from your conversation with the prospect and your Internet research to see if there are any colorful anecdotes or stories you can incorporate into the presentation. Consider finding an anecdote that illustrates the objectives and mission of the company.

Finally, consider the news. Is there a way to tie a client-centered current event into your presentation? This gives you an incredible advantage, as it firmly positions you as a someone who is quick, up to date, agile and tuned into to their specific words.

Presenting to Prospects and Peers

The moment has arrived! Pay close attention to the simple, basic, but very important nonverbal aspects of your presentation.

Chief among them is the handshake. You want to give a firm handshake that indicates your solid, stable nature. Have you seen an advertisement for Allstate insurance? The image is a pair of cupped hands and the logo "you are in good hands with Allstate."

You never get a second chance to make a first impression.

What you radiate is important. You want to telegraph a number of messages, but of primary importance is how easy it is to deal with you. Remember, many products and services are similar, so what can really differentiate you from the pack is the "you" factor. Being likable is a small part, but you must also radiate being trustworthy, competent, and willing to go the extra mile to deliver exceptional customer service.

Names Are Key

Can you remember and pronounce the names of all your clients? This is important for two reasons. First, most people respond positively to the sound of their names. Today's era of personalized email is a prime example of this.

Second, according to ancient legend, once you know someone's name, you have a certain power or influence over them. In fact, folklore is filled with stories about mythical and terrifying beasts that can be rendered harmless simply by discovering their name and saying it aloud.

Use your clients' names in the course of your presentation for added personalization.

Verify Verify Verify

In speaking about his talks with the Russians, President Regan coined the phrase "trust, but verify."

This is excellent advice to all presenters.

Before you begin your introduction, you want to verify that you are both on the same page. Maybe just hours have passed since you confirmed the meeting, it is a mistake to automatically make the assumption that the amount of time you have to spend together and the key topic to discuss are the same. Check for any breaking news about your prospect or a related business.

Are We On Target With Time?

You scheduled the presentation for a certain amount of time, let's say an hour. When you arrive at the site of the presentation, verify you have the hour initially agreed upon.

Why? If there is an emergency on the client's side, you will be able to launch into your short version (you did create a fallback short version, didn't you) that takes into account the three key points, or you can ask the client which of the points you planned to discuss are they most interested in.

Second, if the time has changed for whatever reason, this should raise a red flag. Sure, emergencies do happen and there are always fires to put out, but it's worth it to ask if anything has changed since the two of you last spoke.

For example, it's possible that the client ran your idea or product by a superior and learned that your idea or product is not of interest any longer. Perhaps s/he's still taking your meeting as a courtesy, but is no longer in a buying mode. Time is too precious a commodity for all parties involved and accepting the courtesy and being brief may very well be of value in the future.

At this point, it may be a good idea to be direct and ask if anything has changed you should know about.

Are We On Target With The Subject?

We automatically assume, of course we are on target. This is the purpose of the setting the meeting in the first place.

One of the best ways to make verifications is to do so informally. For example, perhaps the client will meet you in the lobby and escort you to his or her office. As you make small talk, go ahead and slip in a very casual, "so, just confirming we have the hour to discuss (x,y,z)."

Make No Assumptions About Your Audience

Bob, a portfolio manager, had been chatting up a room of clients, giving them proprietary information about his company. After the meeting broke up, he was shocked to hear that one of the individuals he assumed was an employee had instead been a competitor who earlier gave a presentation of his own.

How do you find out who's in the room? And how do you handle "ears" that aren't supposed to be there?

One tactic is to ask everyone to introduce himself or herself. If competitors reveal themselves, don't visibly react, but do keep the proprietary information to yourself as you deliver the presentation. Later call the client, explain you felt uncomfortable speaking in front of someone who is or could be a potential competitor, and that you would like to schedule another meeting.

It's also a good idea to ask the client if anyone else in the company should attend. Even if the short notice won't allow for this, you will have a name and contact information. You can then email or overnight the material you covered.

The Presentation

So, now that you've verified everything you possibly can, restate the purpose for making the presentation. Something like "Jim, two weeks ago we chatted about some of your company's needs and how my ABC Corporation can help. In the time we have, I'd like to stress *three ways* of how we can help you."

Why Limit Yourself to Three Key Points?

Statistics reveal that people generally only comprehend three key points before encountering sensory overload. Also you won't simply be delivering the "point" in a sentence, but rather, will use the points as broad headers for topics that support your focused meeting.

Support with Anecdotes, Facts, and Statistics

Each key point should be supported with a mix of statistics, facts, and anecdotes. Of the three, anecdotes and short, vivid stories will be the most welcome and appreciated. In an effort to help a client understand how they hand select stocks and bonds for individual portfolios, a portfolio manager might support a key point by saying he is like a celebrity chef, choosing the freshest market ingredients for just the right offering.

Just as you can help your audience understand your talk by using all of the three key modalities (auditory, visual, kinesthetic) if you include statistics as well as stories, you can increase comprehension and credibility.

Anecdotal stories broaden the spectrum for your audience so they can map the story to their own experience.

The Summary: Reinforcing Key Benefits

Here is where you reiterate your client's objective, recap your three key points, reinforce how your plan provides the solutions the client desires, and wrap it up in a way that naturally segues into the open-ended question period that is to follow.

This is the section where you have the opportunity to really understand your client's objectives, and ask the kind of pointed, open ended questions that provoke honest, revealing answers that help you plan an effective close.

Summaries are what they imply. Your summary should reaffirm your commitment to the client. One way to do this is restate the clients objectives. Answer each of the client's objectives with one of your three key points. You will be able to weave the two together, reaffirming your unique capability to work together to the desired goal.

Conquering Possible Sales Objections

When CEO's are interviewed by the media, they are carefully coached on creative ways to answer the questions they do not want to be asked! The same tactic is used in the White House, where all the president's men (and women) are asked by the press secretary to write the most objectionable question they could think of as a media person.

By preparing for difficult questions in advance, CEO's, politicians, and everyone who's on the spot can sound cool, calm, and collected as they answer. Neglecting to prepare is short sighted behavior.

Realistically, most companies can compete on price, quality, or customer service. Rarely can a company compete on all three.

So be honest with yourself. What is your strength? What does the client want?

If your weakness is price, and you know the client to buy on price, how will you address this issue?

Prepare in advance, perhaps brainstorming some "freebies" you can throw into the deal that allows you to keep your price but makes the client feel as if he or she is getting more than they are paying for.

As you listen to the objection, hear the prospect out and rephrase the question to make sure you heard it correctly. If the objection was emotional, respond to this first, then answer the objection with your prepared statement for hidden value benefits. Be certain to close your statement on a positive note, painting a vivid mental picture for the client or what they will receive and experience as a result of doing business with you.

Call To Action

You've taken the time to carefully qualify your client for your product or service. You've taken extra steps to find your client's hidden objectives. If you've been listening intently, you know what they want and are primed to deliver.

Assume in your tone and bearing that you will work together. Do not at any time express timidity, or uncertainty, that this sale will close.

If you have successfully positioned yourself as the true solution to their problem, you are in command, even if they haven't yet "officially" made up their mind about engaging you. If you act "as if" you have the deal, they may be inclined to just go with the flow. Have your calendar ready to schedule the next meeting.

In this scenario, attitude is everything.

Tips for Co-Presenting with Colleagues

First, realize that practice is essential. Second, if you habitually divide the presentation into separate roles, be certain you are familiar with your colleague's role in the event they are unexpectedly delayed.

For example, portfolio managers may travel at different times or from different cities to make a client presentation, and a member's plane is delayed. If your colleagues know your role and vice versa, they can cover for you. The presentation message can still be delivered flawlessly.

The strongest advice I can personally offer is to clearly demonstrate respect for your client or colleague by focusing, even lavishing, attention on them as they speak.

Yes, this requires a bit of acting. After all, you've heard your colleague speak dozens if not hundreds of times before.

But lavishing attention on your colleague accomplishes several key issues, all of which work together to win you the deal.

First, it shows a united front.

Second, when you radiate a sense of confidence in your colleague, clients sense it. They think, wow, if the colleague is so enamored of this person's ideas, this firm must really be great.

Of course, you would expect that your colleague would reciprocate and lavish the same attention on you when you are presenting.

Positive Energy is Key

Mary, 23, is a San Francisco based analyst for a financial company. New on the job, she was quickly drafted to go on a road show and give a presentation to various clients. A woman from her company's public relations department was charged with being her guide.

"I was very nervous," she told me. "But what saved the day was the way the PR woman would just smile and beam at me as I addressed the clients. She didn't say a word, but the way she focused her positive attention on me really filled me with confidence!"

When you present, note your colleague's behavior. Do they look out the window, or flick their pen? Or do they radiate positive energy?

Make a pact to support one another in the same way Mary was supported, and you will see the results you desire.

Presenting to Colleagues

Quite often we take the most important people in our life for granted. This possibly accounts for the high rate of divorce in America, and also, why many feel they do not get the career promotions they deserve.

A common perception is that it's "okay" to "run an idea" a colleague or a superior. After all, she isn't a client! We tend to focus on perfecting our presentations to prospects and clients to the depth of our ability, arguing that this is where the money is.

Think again.

Whether you realize it or not, you have a certain stature in your industry.

Your stature is a result of what clients say about you, in addition to how you are regarded by peers.

Often, you may be in a situation where you need a peer's help or support. Even if the two of you are good friends or lunch buddies, reconsider a casual approach when it comes to presenting your ideas. Instead, use the same professional approach you would use for a prospective client.

Formal Presentations Set a Stage for Mutual Respect

Respect is a two way street. By formally scheduling and rehearsing a presentation for your peer or superior, you are establishing respect on many levels.

First, you are setting the groundwork for respect for your idea, even at its present ephemeral stage. Marriages ideally last a lifetime, and most people try to start off on the right foot by going through the traditional steps and having a formal ceremony. True, some people elope and go on to have healthy marriages, but spur of the moment decisions rarely are taken seriously.

Second, by giving your colleague or superior a formal presentation, you are also articulating your respect for them and their time.

And finally, you are showing respect for yourself.

A good rule of thumb is to follow the steps you already follow for a prospect or client presentation.

This may include a PowerPoint presentation printed out as a handout, so that you can be on target with points and the audience can take notes. One financial advisor I know sends a PowerPoint presentation as an email, so that her ideas have a distinctive look and easy to read bullet point design.

Walking Softly and Carrying a Big Stick

When presenting to colleagues and superiors you want to also keep your tone friendly and business casual. You want to sound natural, yet at the same time, have the ammunition in terms of facts, statistics, and anecdotes to back it all up.

You have heard me say this numerous times, but perception is everything. By preparing yourself so completely for what is typically a "casual" presentation places you miles ahead of the pack.

Summary:

☑ Create a presentation template that suits your business and your personal style;

☑ Incorporate open-ended questions & Internet research as you prepare;

☑ Brand yourself against the competition via customization;

☑ Identify a (client) need and fill it;

☑ Use your prospect's corporate "buzz words" & current events in presentation;

☑ Verify time and subject before launching into your presentation;

☑ Make sure competitors are not in the room as you present;

☑ Clients are impressed when you "actively listen";

☑ Summarize by acting "as if" you already have the deal.

Assignments:

1. Determine your company's strength (price, quality, customer service) and which of these three it would be difficult to compete on.

2. Create a series of qualifying questions to zero in on what your prospect most values in what you have to sell.

3. Consider your competitive advantage and create a series of responses designed to bring the prospect away from haggling over x (your company's weakness) and bringing them to y (your company's strength).

4. Resolve to improve your presentation skills when it comes to colleagues and superiors.

Chapter 6
Creating a Public Talk

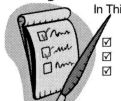

In This Chapter You Will Learn

☑ How to Structure the Talk
☑ How to Motivate Your Audience
☑ The Power of Stories & Anecdotes

"I'm a great believer in luck, and I find the harder I work the more I have of it."
Thomas Jefferson (1743 - 1826)

"I need to attract more business," one of Boston's many independent financial planners told me over coffee at Starbucks. "And I hear public talks are a good way to attract potential clients."

Yes, a public talk is an excellent way to find prospective clients. It is also an excellent way of enhancing your image, giving credibility to your business, and getting your name into the media.

You might also find yourself in need of public speaking skills if you speak in front of your industry's trade organization or on behalf of a non-profit group. And yes, if you want to translate your professional experience into a book, you must give public talks to create interest and boost sales.

At its core, this chapter addresses tips, tricks, and techniques to wow a diverse crowd assembled to hear you speak on a topic of your expertise. It may be financial planning, or the topic may be the obscure issue of how to avoid shark attacks while surfing off the coast of Bora Bora. In both scenarios, participants have a keen interest in what you have to say -- but only in terms of your talks' impact on their lives.

Behind Every Power Player is an Effective Speaker

The earliest recorded material on public speaking is entitled *The Instruction of Ptah-hotep and the Instruction of Keg' Emmi*, an ancient book discovered on the banks of the Nile River in Egypt. The book advises power-seekers on how to influence kings and satisfy their political desires by developing a silver tongue.

Speaking holds much of that same role today, but the flowery eloquence of rhetorical tradition has given way to short, powerfully sculpted talks with a firm outline and vivid examples.

Audience attention has truncated to the point that we must continuously work to paint appropriate word pictures to underscore key concepts. To do this effectively we must be as clear and concise as possible.

Good speakers deliver content, but deliver it in a way tailored for the ear. When speakers are solely concerned with communicating their content, the effect is similar to a director shooting several reels of film, and sending it to the theaters to screen "as is."

For example, in the film industry, executives screen "dailies" each day. A "daily" is the raw, uncut, unedited work of a director for that day's shoot. Think of a raw, uncut diamond before an experienced jeweler creates the facets that make the diamond sparkle and shine. Yes, the executives are getting the "content" which will become a hit movie like *The Godfather* and the jeweler is about to set work on an engagement ring that can cost hundreds of thousands of dollars, but it's "raw content."

An expert in his or her field may feel that delivering "raw content" is enough. After all, the expert feels he is at the cutting edge of research in their industry, and may feel he is doing a favor to the audience by disseminating this raw information.

Remember that we live in a package-conscious society.

Supermarket shelves are filled with hundreds of variety of soap, yet savvy marketers know they have to do more than just put a lumpy bar of fat on a shelf. Each soap has its own "story" which is telegraphed via its packaging. *Caress Soap* is pink and appeals to women, even without reading the copy on the soap box. *Irish Spring* is a "manly scent" and the green of the box, plus the name "spring" make us feel clean and renewed.

The "content" is the same for all brands (i.e. soap), but what keeps us in the supermarket looking at the various boxes is the way the content is packaged.

When we speak, this "packaging" is translated into tailoring our message for the human ear using the techniques I've described.

The Audience Wants You To Be Great!

In the speaking world, enthusiasm and the willingness to make a personal connection with your audience can make up for a multitude of transgressions. Speakers who focus exclusively on content are often in for a surprise when they discover that what audiences really want most is someone who understands their needs, and delivers solutions in the most clear, concise and entertaining way possible.

Consider your own experience in school. Some teachers bored you to tears while others excited your curiosity to learn. The truth about most boring teachers, and presenters, is that they have never understood the importance of stepping outside themselves to see how their message is delivered and more importantly, received.

Experienced speakers, even intuitive beginning speakers, quickly "feel" the energy in the room. The energy is present as a "buzz" as the audience settles into their seats, excited that the speaker will answer questions and issues they have about the topic.

You've been there, in the audience, with that same expectation, haven't you?

It's natural for energy levels to ebb and flow. In fact, this is desirable because it replicates the experience of "real life." When screenwriters develop movies, they do so with an eye toward the roller coaster experience of real life, with its moments of intense excitement and expectation, the afternoon lull, inflamed passion, and template-driven productivity.

Monitoring the energy in the room is of primary importance for any speaker. When the talk is over, over ninety percent of your content will be forgotten. By the end of the week, you will be lucky if they remember a single point you made, let alone your name.

What the audience will remember, however, is the connection you made with them.

Divining Audience Expectations

The key to successful presentations lies in devoting a few moments of quality time in analyzing who the audience will be, and what they have come to hear. Audiences come to seminars for a variety of reasons. The more you can analyze what motivated your audience to attend the more successful you will be.

If you are giving a talk to members of a specific company, your job is much easier. Why? You have a solid understanding of why you have been engaged and what you are expected to deliver. Also, you have the added advantage of questioning audience members beforehand about what they specifically want to know.

Ask the meeting planner far in advance of your talk if you can chat with a few key individuals to better focus your talk to that audience. You want to ask what specific challenges they are facing that you can help resolve. If you can use any specific examples in the course of your talk, you will automatically lock in more audience interest.

If you are speaking on a more general nature, be certain that your talk is "you-centric." This means, it includes ways that your audience can improve their lives.

For inspiration, take a look at the headlines on most glossy magazines. Everyone wants a miracle diet that allows them to look svelte and eat as much as possible, have better sex, meet the partner of their dreams, and increase their wealth.

Spend some time considering what you and your talk have to offer, and how you can marry these benefits with the core desires of your audience. This virtually guarantees a successful talk!

Translating the Written Word

As I explained in the previous chapter, you must communicate with your audience using your body as well as your voice.

When it comes to addressing audiences, you might consider employing some of the vocal tricks you would use as if reading stories to children. This may include varying your voice in terms of pitch, vocal variety, and/or using a "character voice" if appropriate. For example, this can include imitating a customer if you are giving a talk on customer service – or imitating any voice to represent a conversation in your talk.

Imitating a "customer" can be very effective for sales talks. When I give talks to sales teams, I enjoy preparing my list of "customer types" in advance and using them for role model exercises. It breaks up the "official feel" of the talk and generates both fun and learning in participants.

When it comes to finding the right story or imagery, remember the film industry and try to tap into a universal experience. On television, sit-coms attract a wide audience because whether the characters are family members or co-workers, we can relate to them and their situations.

It's wise to use stories that bring emotion into play. Kodak, the film and camera company, sells a fairly generic product. It's difficult to get worked up about a roll of film. However, in their advertising Kodak highlights not their product but the emotion their product creates via the abilty to record images and thus create a lasting memory.

Recall the last time you were alone with a television and a remote control. As you surfed from channel to channel, chances are you stopped to take a longer look at a scene that had some emotional resonance that drew you to linger and see how things turned out. Once again taking a cue from the entertainment industry, it's important to recognize that no scene in a script can move forward without conflict or heated emotion: it is what captures your interest and propels the story forward. You will do well to incorporate this into your talks.

Why Stories Mesmerize

Audiences love stories and anecdotes. They provide a spot of color in an otherwise dry presentation. In addition, they help the listener map the story to their own experience. Finally, stories and anecdotes can underscore the key point.

Stories are of such importance that if you feel you need to loosen up a bit or become a better storyteller, consider taking a class in theater at your local adult education center. While you probably won't be acting a story out, audiences do enjoy it when you tell a story as if you are reliving the experience, allowing them to get a vivid sense of your experience and impersonating the characters involved.

Transitions to stories should be natural. Many speakers simply end on a key point, and begin their story with something like "...so I was standing on the porch of my mother's house." This technique immediately transports the audience to your story without an awkward explanation of what you are doing.

Nido Qubein, former president of the National Speakers Association, is highly regarded as a master storyteller. When sharing his wisdom with newer speakers, he explains that it is important to make stories as vivid as possible, and to also make sure that the audience you're speaking to can personally relate to them.

Quebein's point is well taken. Just a few months ago in Boston, I attended a seminar in which a financial guru spoke to several webmasters who were sole practitioners and heads of their own company. Assuming those in attendance were far wealthier than they were in reality, the financial guru gave the kind of figures and situations the attendees would experience if they were millionaires, not the struggling entrepreneurs they were. As a result, the attendees couldn't relate and the emotional connection was broken.

Begin Formulating Your Talk With the End In Mind

One of the common mistakes presenters make is that they focus 90% of their energy on the content of the talk, perhaps 9%

on the introduction, and — if the thought even occurs to them --
give 1% of their attention to the close of their speech.

Wrong move.

The close is actually the most powerful element of your entire
talk. It's the summation of your ideas, and the call of action that
has the possibility of burning you forever into the mind of
attendees.

I urge you to consider writing and rehearsing your conclusion
first. Once that's perfected, turn your attention to writing and
rehearsing the opening.

Then, when you're satisfying you have a compelling opening
and powerful close that will strongly motivate your audience to
action, work on supporting the conclusion through the points
you will discuss in the body of your talk.

In real life, we strive to create an attractive parting shot. We
pay careful attention to dress when we're going to a formal or
important event. We buy nice cars so we give a good impression
as we drive off or arrive. We try to live in the best neighborhood
we can afford. In fact, many people embark on crash diets before
weddings, so everyone will remember a "slim image."

So ask yourself, since the end of a talk is what everyone
remembers, why is the close often delivered in a rushed, exhausted,
just-ran-out-of-steam sort of way? Many speakers actually act as if
a great burden has been lifted from them as they race to conclude
their talk, gather their notes, and heave a heavy sigh of relief as
they run from the podium.

Not an attractive parting shot, is it?

Watch for these behaviors in others, and in yourself. Make
sure you pace yourself so that your presentation isn't rushed.
And if it is, don't show it. Cut out the least important part of
your conclusion always remembering to stay cool, calm, and
collected.

Above all, remember that in every scenario, but especially when
you want to reinforce that impression of being powerful and in
control, the pause is your friend. Even if the meeting planner is
frantically signaling you from the back of the room you're out of

time, cut your words, but keep your pause. Wrap up in fifteen seconds, and leave the podium slowly with your head held high.

The audience won't think anything amiss, and I, for one, will be quite proud of you!

A Quick, Crucial Note About Question & Answer Period

In keeping with the idea of leaving the podium with a powerful image, make sure that you never, ever end your presentation or talk with the question and answer period. If you do so, you risk leaving your image dependant on the last person who asked a question. It could very well be unflattering, or it might raise some doubt in the audience's mind.

The best technique is to announce that you will hold a brief period for questions, and then make your closing remarks. Be certain to cut off questions at the appropriate time so you can deliver your powerful conclusion as rehearsed.

Opening Your Talk with Pizzazz

So there they are, your audience, peeking at you with a curious mix of expectation and excitement. In restaurant lingo, your first few words are the audience's amuse bouche, the complimentary, creatively prepared and presented "starter appetizer" which gives a taste or hint of the talents yet to come.

Chefs in fine restaurants spend a great deal of time developing the amuse bouche, because they know from experience that when they dazzle the diner before the main course, the "mystery" is taken out of the equation and the diner can just sit back, forget about making a judgment, and enjoy.

The opening of your talk serves the same purpose. Your objective is multifold, but the top three goals are:

☑ Motivate the audience to like you and give them a reason to trust you;

☑ Introduce the theme of your message and how applying your message will help them accomplish their goals;

☑   To put the audience at ease to participate in the exchange of energy.

Many presenters pride themselves on a "no nonsense" approach to public speaking. They feel as if they are performing an informational service, and that content is the most important element, overlooking delivery. They would do well to think again.

Research has proven time and again that listeners won't hear your content if they haven't yet come to like or trust you as an individual. Many presenters have found that just taking a few simple steps, such as chatting with the audience beforehand, smiling, and making sure you explain that you are accessible after the talk and later, by email (providing you are willing to do this) can make all the difference. As I have said, your audience is sizing you up long before you formally utter the first words.

Your opening lines depend a great deal on your subject and your personality. One particularly effective beginning is to sum up a sense of the audience's frustration, deep longing, or pain, and then explain how by the end of the talk you will have given them the tools to solve their problems.

For a moment, assume you are going to give a talk on weight loss. Perhaps you would begin by emphasizing with the audience how hard it is to lose weight, maybe even speak about your own battles of the bulge. Using very vivid word imagery, you'd describe the tortuous exercise, the starvation diets, and the maddening frustration of seeing those pounds creep back up.

Then -- you discovered the three-part secret that had the pounds melting away like butter and gave you the slim, trim figure you are showing off today!

As you can imagine, you'd have your audience hooked with this opening (assuming they are all overweight and anxious to hear a solution).

This framework can work for a wide variety of talks. Simply plug in the subject. Now, assume that you've written a book on overcoming writer's block, and the audience is full of aspiring writers. As with the weight loss opening, sum up the frustration of being a blocked writer, really make those long hours hunched over the computer as vivid as possible. Make the audience relive the pain of time spent at the keyboard with nothing to show for it. Then hit them with the promise of relief! Explain how you too felt their pain, but now, you've written twelve bestsellers and, before the night is finished, you will reveal your secrets to them!

Even the subject of investments can fit into this formula. Make the audience relieve the frustration of having money slip through their fingers. Strike terror in their hearts by telling them the horrific future that awaits them if they neglect to save. Then tantalize them with the promise of indescribable riches if they listen to your advice (you will also have to give evidence of how you turned your financial life around or how, thanks to the advice you will give them, you are living high on the hog).

On a verbal or subconscious level, you also want to telegraph the following information in these opening moments:

1. Listening to your talk will be well worth their time;
2. The talk will be enjoyable and educational;
3. You will deliver what they came to hear: solutions.

Covering the Basics

Who will make your introduction? A good introduction gives you unofficial third party endorsement that enhances your authority to speak on the topic, and generates attention. If you don't know your introducer, it's a good idea to meet with them beforehand and make sure they know how to pronounce your name, etc.

Many speakers have learned the hard way to take certain precautions, such as printing out an introduction and taking it with them to the talk (even though it had already been mailed or emailed). Another idea is to create a generic introduction on your web site, so it can be grabbed from the web in a pinch.

Then again, there's always the possibility that you will take a look at your presenter, and realize that you'd be much better off introducing yourself!

Self-Introductions: A Case Study

Les Brown is an internationally recognized motivational speaker who addresses Fortune 500 companies. He is also a highly skilled self-introducer.

Aware of the possibility that an audience might pre-judge him because he's African-American, Brown has scripted a humorous intro. In it he hints at the talk to come and gives the audience the opportunity for a few chuckles, manages to name the brand name companies who hire him to motivate their sales force, and even sprinkles his intro with the names of other famous speakers he's shared the dais with.

What the audience wants to hear in an introduction is:

1. A friendly, engaging tone;
2. Your credentials (make them as impressive as possible while factual).
3. Why you are the perfect speaker for this topic and this audience.

Summary:

☑ From ancient history to today, speaking mastery is a road to prestige and power;

☑ Audiences want you to be great and are supportive of you;

☑ Create visual and verbal signposts for easier audience navigation;

☑ Begin with the finale in mind;

☑ Your opening serves as a "taste" of your tone and message;

☑ Anecdotes help the audience map your message to their experience.

Assignments:

1. Decide to tell a story in your next presentation. As you practice, make it as dramatic and powerful as possible.

2. Consider the next talk you plan to give. This time, turn the table by creating and rehearsing your finale first. Make it as strong and motivating as possible.

3. For the same talk, plan your opening as you simultaneously envision an "amuse bouche" or creatively prepared appetizer at a fine dining restaurant. How can you use creativity to create the same excitement and anticipation for your talk as the chef does with his or her cuisine?

4. Create a universal introduction that can be slanted to fit virtually any talk you might give. Post it on your web so that it can be accessed by your introducer in a pinch.

Chapter 7
Connecting with Your Audience

In This Chapter You Will Learn

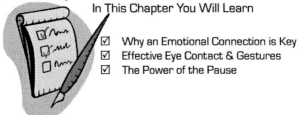

☑   Why an Emotional Connection is Key
☑   Effective Eye Contact & Gestures
☑   The Power of the Pause

"The meeting of two personalities is like the contact of two chemical substances: if there is any reaction, both are transformed."

Carl Jung (1875 - 1961)

Have you thought about the reasons you enjoy a movie rather than most lectures? Even if the topic is one of personal interest or on a target subject in our industry, most people would rather see the movie.

Why?

Speakers are limited to certain tools, including PowerPoint slides, white boards, and props. Highly effective speakers tap into vocal variety, gestures, and the power of the pause to help transmit their message.

Movies make much use of sound, and have many other high tech tools to engage the viewer. More succinctly, movies focus on "emotion" whereas a presenter seeks to transmit knowledge or information.

Making an Emotional Connection

The art of movie making is just about a century old, the fathers of our industry intuitively knew that an audience must have an emotional connection with the stories and characters for a film to do well also keep the audience wanting to keep coming back.

In other words, the audience must "feel" connected to you, as if they can identify with you and the concepts you are articulating, as if in a movie.

Interestingly, it's not just your words that influence your audience, but the fact that you are saying them. The more you connect with your audience, the more your audience will be swept up in not just your words, but relate to your message, and buy the ideas you are selling.

Secrets of the Spoken Message

Most of us are masters at making ourselves shine on the printed page. After all, we are experts in our field, have credentials to back up what we say, and take pride in what we achieved.

But writing a well-received paper versus giving a well-received presentation, are very different entities.

Why?

Because the process of "speaking the message" and "creating the message" are separate arts. Listeners understand spoken messages in a different way than readers understand the written word.

Spoken Words Vs. Text

When one "hears" a message the brain must work harder to comprehend the information, process it, and store it in an appropriate "mental folder" in a fleetingly quick period of time. Statistics reveal that people talk ten times faster than most listeners can comprehend.

Listening to a spoken message in a seminar environment means that other stimuli are competing for your attention at the same time. There's no chance to turn back and review.

Appeal to Audience Modalities: Function As a Giant Yellow Highlighter

Can you imagine getting through university days without your fat yellow highlighter? This useful device served several key functions.

☑   When the entire dorm or library was full of noise and activity, holding it in your hand helped you focus your attention on the text and block outside distractions;

☑   When you were cramming for an exam, you probably had an instinctive sense of what would be on the test because you would use your highlighter to underline the material you really needed to focus upon;

☑   Finally, if you were a very effective highlighter, you would be able to excerpt text to form a very succinct outline of the chapter.

The audience for your presentation is filled with people who understand things within different modalities. You must

"transcribe" the conceptual idea so it can be understood in a visual, auditory, and kinesthetic manner.

You've heard people remark a colleague is a "good speaker."   The praise is directly related to how well the speaker used visual, auditory, and kinesthetic elements in the talk.   These elements are often referred to as the "Three Modalities."

How do you do this? First, use your voice to reflect a change of subject through your tone and repetition (auditory). Vocalize, specifically where you are in your mental outline. For example, "today I would like to discuss three key points." Then list the points, and before you discuss point one, verbalize "So, to start, let's consider Point One."

Use gestures to add a visual signpost (visual). In the above scenario, you might want to raise the fingers of your hand to illustrate the three points you will speak on. When you come to point one, raise that finger as you verbally say "Point One." Slides and exercises (kinesthetic) round out the effectiveness of your presentation. By functioning as a highlighter in voice, repetition, and gesture, you help your audience understand your message.

Creating Units of Information

When you make clear definitions between your points you are creating chunks. Chunks are self-contained units of information. Each chunk is headed by your key point and supported by your colorful assortment of anecdotes, statistics, and facts. What's great about chunks is that they are easy for you to remember, and easy for your audience to remember as well.

To further reinforce that each "chunk" is a separate unit of information, pause briefly, and then clearly state: "So, now that we've finished point #1, we will address #2" or whatever words you prefer to use to show this clear deliniation. This is especially important when you finish with the final story of your first "chunk" and prepare to launch into your second point.

Presentation Secrets of Hollywood Hit Films and Top Politicians

In Hollywood, screenwriters create the message. Actors verbalize the message in a dramatic, emotional way.

In politics, speechwriters create the message. Politicians deliver the message in a commanding, forceful manner that strikes through to the heart of their audience.

You are an executive, an entrepreneur, the owner of a small business, or a writer who realizes that the quickest way up the ladder of success is to "speak" your message rather than use reams and reams of paper.

Where many people err is thinking that to be an effective presenter, all one has to do is read aloud the crafted message.

And we've all been there, right? We've attended a presentation when all the speaker did was read their notes?

No eye contact.

No gestures.

Rigid stance as they grip the podium.

A great presentation is fundamentally different from just reading text.

To drive this concept closer to home, let's consider the average financial quantitative analyst or portfolio manager. Most of them have advanced scientific degrees and are truly experts. Yet when they start talking numbers, few outside their field would even have an inkling of what they're talking about.

This is problematic in a presentation because the expert is giving a series of numbers, without providing the context for the information. Yes, everyone understands why he is there, but before

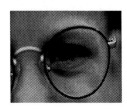

the audience can truly listen they must be engaged and a connection must be made as to what those numbers represent.

Studies reflect that in the first several minutes of any presentation, the audience is not "hearing you."

They are determining on a subconscious and nonverbal basis whether or not they can trust you, if you are on the same wavelength, and if they even want to do business with you. All this assessment is before they will begin paying attention to your analytic material.

A good analogy is that of a computer with a fast modem but a dead phone connection. You have all the resources to communicate, but the critical connection is just not present.

An actor without any understanding of the analytics that go into this kind of presentation, would know how to proceed. He would first create an emotional connection by bringing the minds of the attendees back to the core message: the need to provide a safe pension fund for the company's employees. Perhaps the actor may describe an employee by name and ask pointed questions about what could happen if the pension fund faltered.

"So our employee, Joe Smith, thinks he's set because his pension fund can carry him through retirement because his house is paid off and has appreciated in value over the years. But all at once, several things happen. First, his wife becomes ill and a second mortgage is taken to pay off her medical expenses. Then, Joe's daughter gets married -- more money from the house.

The long appreciation ends, and the house shrinks in value at the same time that his daughter's husband leaves her and their young child. Two more dependents to feed and shelter, and now, educate. Maybe he hadn't been counting on his company's retirement fund to see him through retirement, but now, it's all he has. Is it enough? More important, will it always be there when he needs it?"

Once an emotional connection is made, the facts and figures can be presented to support how your company's option is more effective than the plan currently in place, and then talk hard numbers in earnest.

Regardless of the type of presentation you are making, connecting initially on an emotional level is key in making the topic relative to the audience.

Power Surge: Connecting Through Eye Contact, Gestures, Movement, and the Pause

If the most important aspect of connecting with your audience was reading them your presentation, all you'd really need to do is send an audio tape or CD

What separates a presentation from a vocal reading is not just that the presentation is live, but that your have additional communication tools and your availability to the audience.

The best way to connect with your audience is when you speak directly to them. Naturally, there is an art to referencing from notes while giving the effect of extemporaneous speaking. This involves a certain amount of upfront practice and preparation, but once mastered, you will be able to effortlessly reference notes while remaining fully engaged with your audience.

Many executives and entrepreneurs today lack the time to practice memorization and delivery. Their focus is on delivery high content information and persuasive presentations, but naturally want to connect as much as possible with their audience.

The Eyes Have It

You've heard it said that the eyes are the windows to our soul. Many people claim they can look into the eyes of another and sense if they are telling the truth.

In the Old West, a stranger with "shifty eyes" was quickly run out of town -- or shot!

Presidential candidates with shifty eyes don't make it past the primaries.

When you present, the audience will be looking at you, often directly meeting your eyes. It's important to cement that connection by returning their gaze.

You may assume when presenters are just beginning to speak, eye contact is intimidating. But on the contrary, making eye contact is an excellent way to relax you and charge your presentation with added warmth and personality.

The trick is seeing the assembled group as your friend.

One great way to do this is to arrive a bit early, whether it's for a presentation or a public talk, and chit chat a bit with the crowd. If you are giving a public talk, why not pass around handouts, introducing yourself as you do so.

When you speak, seek these people out and as you make eye contact with them, silently telegraph positive energy and good wishes.

You will find the result rather gratifying because when you make eye contact with just one person as you speak, others interpret the connection as if it is meant for them as well.

Suddenly, you will find that more and more people in the audience will look at you with encouragement, caught up in all the positive energy that is going around. Your mission is also self serving because when you connect with as many of this type as possible, you collect the positive energy and radiate it back towards the audience.

Select people who are smiling, nodding their heads in agreement, and appear to be listening with full attention.

Radiating positive energy is also important in a smaller presentation context. Again, be certain to look at everyone in the group, not just the person perceived to be the decision maker. Aside from the fact that avoidance of eye contact may be perceived as rude, looking at everyone covers you if you are uncertain who is the decision maker.

Often, decisions are made by committee, and chances are high that everyone in the room will have their turn at commenting on your presentation. If you neglect to be an equal eye contact presenter, even out of nervousness, it's possible someone may resent you for overlooking them and hold it against you later.

Effective Use of Notes

For a moment, consider your favorite newscasters. Each day, they are presented with new tragedies. They must convey each story as emotionally compelling as possible to maintain you as a viewer.

What is the number one thing that newscasters must do effectively?

Speak clearly? Maybe. Speak without stumbling over words? Obviously.

But the most important thing in their minds is making that emotional connection with the viewer. They know that once the audience senses they "don't care" or "act superior," they will change the channel. It's as easy as that.

Newscasters read a different script each broadcast. In the event you are in the position of having to give a new talk every day, don't feel as if you must rehearse it and rehearse it as you do a prepared speech.

Investing time in rehearsals during your first few speeches, especially on video tape (or lacking that, audio tape) is a great tool to help you with confidence and delivery.

Formatting Your Talking Points

The initial stages of preparing talking points are very similar to preparing computer outlines. In both cases, you begin with key elements:

1. Analysis of what the audience wants, and why they want it from you;

2. Analysis of who the audience is and at what level they will comprehend your information;

3. Analysis of length. You want to talk for the shortest time period that will enable then to clearly absorb your three key points, and see a direct application of how they can immediately apply your information to their lives.

Preparation for Presenters
Step One

Since you are an expert in your field and can most likely recall anecdotes without having to read them, type the key points in the CENTER of a large piece of letter-size paper.

Use a large font size, such as 16 or 18, and make sure there is plenty of margin on both sides.

If possible, try to group points together, so that ideas are contained on one page. The reason for this is that pages can and do get separated, and while an audience might not notice the introduction of a new topic, they will notice a non-sequiter or a thought awkwardly divided at the end of a page.

Step Two

Rehearse and commit to memory your introduction and conclusion, as well as your three key points. You must make your opening engaging and your conclusion powerful.

Holding Your Notes

You do not want to use your notes as a prop.

I have mentioned the value of videotaping your practice sessions. On review, you can see yourself emerging as a professional newscaster in just a few practiced sessions.

If you are speaking from a lectern, leave the notes on the lectern.

If you will hold them in your hand, beware the fan effect!

This is when a case of the jitters causes you to wave the notes around in the air, effectively taking the audience's focus from you to those flying sheets of paper.

As you finish a point, bring your notes up, scan that large-font headline, and lower your notes before beginning.

Why?

So you can focus on your audience!

You might also experiment on video tape or before the mirror with the "slide" method of changing pages (my recommendation) vs. the "flip."

The Audience Bond Is Everything

Your audience will forgive you looking at your notes if you look at them while you speak. In doing so, you are "disconnecting" from your audience. They will feel as if they could have had the document faxed to them. Speaking is more than the spoken word. It is a form of connecting with a group of people, and conveying your ideas from the heart.

The Newscaster Template

Begin with your introduction -- after all, you practiced it at home and know it by heart. Then, if and when you need to be prompted, look at the sheet on your lectern or lift the sheet in your hand, and quickly grasp the segment from your talking point. Speak as much as you can without looking down. You want to actually make the statement directly to one or two people in the audience with eye contact.

Just as you pause for a breath, you want to reference your notes between making key statements.

Smiles Telegraph Positive Energy

In terms of connecting to your audience, a warm, welcoming smile is as important as good eye contact. It will immediately elevate your looks, pump up the energy in the room, and make your audience feel welcome.

Similar to eye contact, a smile connects on a subconscious level. First, it makes you automatically feel more confident, and be perceived as more authoritarian than others.

And like a handshake, a smile establishes trust and paves the way to an emotional connection.

A smile suggests, hey, isn't it great that we're sharing this information together?

If you are not much of a smiler, realize that most smilers are made, not born. It begins when you realize all the incredible benefits that await you when you learn to execute this gesture on a regular basis. Suddenly, people are more friendly, you're better looking, and the world is a great place to be.

Gotta Move to Groove

In the silent era of Hollywood films, directors faced the challenge of keeping audience interest high without words. Music helped, but directors quickly discovered that exaggerated movement enlivened the production more effectively.

To energize the audience, keep them focused on what you have to say, and enhance retention of your ideas, you must move!

One of the most impressive displays of movement I've ever seen was at a seminar given by Publisher's Marketing Association. A PR agent name Tami DePalma kicked off her shoes and jumped onto a chair while explaining the importance of connecting with her audience.

Needless to say, the gentleman on the panel who was to speak after her rousing, enthusiastic performance had much to live up to!

With that bold gesture at the end of a long day of seminars, Tami energized the room in more ways than one. First, the unexpected nature of the movement energized people by the surprise factor alone.

Second, in taking that literal leap, while at the same time giving the publicity-hungry audience the tools to create their own PR, Tami was figuratively taking the audience with her on that leap.

Another example of powerful body language was given by a sales trainer during a conference. He wanted to emphasize the way clients often stall when faced with signing on the dotted line.

Here is what he did:

Voice: *"We want to kick it around some."*

Action: He made a show of kicking an invisible ball.

Voice: *"We want to run it up the flagpole"* (i.e. the big boss).

Action: Hands gesturing moving up an invisible flag.

Voice: *"We want to run it by the Coast."*

Action: A "passing" motion (i.e. to another player).

These gestures made his entire presentation! In fact, it was basically the only element I could remember of his entire presentation.

But it added a fun element to break the monotony.

Making your talk interesting to your audience is what it's all about.

Wake 'Em Up!

Listening is a passive and tiring activity. Consider your own reaction to watching a speaker drone on from behind a podium.

No matter how important their message, it is literal work to stay awake and focused.

When you add movement in the form of strong gestures, active eye contact, and deliberate pauses into the mix, you create excitement — or at least, add some level of anticipation to your captive audience.

Podium Gestures

If you still need the safety of the podium, work on strengthening your gestures. I've already discussed the importance of being a human highlighter, and using the fingers of your hand to illustrate key points as you make them.

But consider using powerful gestures to accentuate your point, especially if your talk is of a motivational or impassioned nature.

Let's return to our financial planner. You can add power and interest to your words by reinforcing them with gestures. It can be as easy as holding your hands up using your left hand to illustrate money coming in, and your right hand to show money going out.

Even if you can't think of anything clever to do with your hands, resist the temptation to keep them obediently by your side. Let them flow with the enthusiasm of your words.

But at the same time, I would caution you to avoid the temptation to use your hands to carry out distracting behaviors. This could include shoving them into your pocket and jiggling coins, twirling your hair, or shuffling your notes. As you practice in front of the mirror or videotape, watch to see if you gravitate toward any of these distractions and condition yourself to put a stop to it before you get to the podium.

Power of the Pause

The impact of silence is more powerful than any string of words. This is especially true in our noisy culture, where silence is perceived as a void that always needs to be filled.

Chances are, you've never intentionally paused or considered the power of a pause, which works effectively on many levels.

Like chicken soup, a pause can work a myriad of miracles in a presentation and is good for whatever challenge you happen to be facing.

When you pause, you allow:

1. The audience time to digest the point you just made.

We speak approximately ten times faster than the mind requires to absorb the concept, and find the appropriate "mental folder" in which to place it. When you pause, you effectively give the audience a welcome opportunity to catch up and thoroughly absorb your point.

2. The audience time to map the point to their own experience.

The pause allows us to reflect on the point, and perform a quick mental search relating the point just made to a personal experience.

3. The audience can reflect on the mastery of your words.

At the end of a long seminar, words become a blur. When you take the time to pause, you allow your audience the opportunity to appreciate your wisdom.

4. Your authority and confidence shines through.

A pause bestows majestic power on whoever uses the technique. Like a fine suit, a pause reinforces your more authority.

5. Personal time to think on how to broach your next topic.

Instead of sounding confused and disoriented by grasping for weak "helper words" (uh, like, so) a pause allows you to keep your dignity as you think of how to phrase your objective.

You can also consider the pause your own silent "fire alarm," serving to harness the audience's attention and bring all eyes back to you. All it takes is a three to five second pause, and suddenly, you can hear a pin drop in the room as everyone waits expectantly for your next thought.

The first time you use a pause it's possible you may feel a bit uncomfortable. Resist the urge to fill in the silence with words.

Silence really is golden, and you'll appreciate the pause the very first time you use it in a presentation.

Summary:

☑ Give your presentation a strong emotional connection.

☑ Use your body to help dramatize key points and keep your audience engaged;

☑ Eye contact allows an emotional bond to form with your audience;

☑ It's possible to maintain an audience connection if you read from notes and continue look at your audience;

☑ A smile telegraphs positive energy;

☑ Command respect through the power of the pause.

Assignments:

1.   Every day affords you the opportunity to make eye contact with strangers. The most natural way to start is in a retail situation when you're asking questions of a sales person, preferably, two salespeople so you can switch eye contact.

2. As you practice your next presentation, go overboard when it comes to adding physical movement and gestures. Tape record your presentation, or ask a friend to watch it. You will be surprised to discover that your movement is not as exaggerated as you think.

3. Put sticky post-it notes over the walls in your office or your room. Pretend that each post-it note is a pair of eyes. Practice delivering half a sentence to one note, then finishing with the other. Become accustomed to the rhythm.

4. In your everyday life, practice the pause. Note how effective it is for simple communication and realize the power you will have using it on the podium.

Chapter 8
Successful Visual Presentations

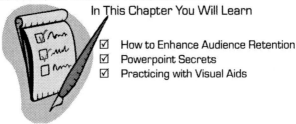

In This Chapter You Will Learn

☑ How to Enhance Audience Retention
☑ Powerpoint Secrets
☑ Practicing with Visual Aids

"An ancient adept has said: 'If the wrong man uses the right means, the right means work in the wrong way. In reality, everything depends on the man and little or nothing on the method."

Carl Jung (1875 - 1961)

In elementary school, we called visual presentations "show and tell." The "showing" was just as important as the "telling" because together, the combination of both "seeing" and "hearing" allowed us to better comprehend the message and increase retention.

Statistics reveal that a typical audience retains just 30% percent of what they hear. Compliment the point with added visual form as they listen, and the number rises 50%. Give the participants physical exercise to reinforce learning, and 70% is retained after three full days.

We've already discussed the fact that people learn in different modalities, so using several modalities in the course of your presentation will enhance learning and reflect well on you as a presenter. Adding visual elements to your presentation also ensures that an audience busy people can grasp the concepts quickly, understand their application, and implement the information immediately.

Almost every type of auxiliary material can be incorporated into your talk or presentation to increase retention and audience involvement. Making presentations visual and interactive makes the material come alive and infuses it with energy. Professional speakers of the entertainment-oriented ilk use music to open their talk as if they were appearing on a late night comedy show. At corporate retreats, team-building songs help employees bond as each new activity or presentation begins.

In this chapter, we will discuss ways to add dazzle with visual aids, group activities, and craft effective handouts to reinforce your message. The most important element to realize is that while visuals are fun, they will never take the place of your natural charisma, concern, and emotional connection with the audience.

PowerPoint: Aid to Understanding

Use of Microsoft's PowerPoint is the most popular of all visual aids. In May of 2002, the Program Director of the Institute of Management Consultants stated that he would no longer bother renting overhead projectors because they are becoming obsolete. In the same memo, he also advised against using flipcharts because few beyond the third row could really see them.

PowerPoint is easy to use and can be used to reinforce message points, yet too often speakers become overly reliant on PowerPoint. While it is true that the auditory and visual message given by a speaker and accompanied by a slide is beneficial because it is reinforced, many use it as an excuse to replace old-fashioned "charisma" with high tech glitz. The danger lies in allowing any visual device to replace the "emotional connection" which is paramount to any presentation.

PowerPoint should be used similar to a chef who ads a sublet nuance to a dish with a small amount of an exotic spice. If the chef dumped in the whole bottle, the nuance would be gone.

A good rule of thumb is no more than twenty slides in the course of an hour's presentation. Certainly no more than one every three minutes. Again, remember your objective with PowerPoint, which is to augment understanding of the key message, and not confuse the issue.

Aids That Can Be Loaded on PowerPoint Slides

Just as variety is the spice of life, it is also the key to an effective PowerPoint presentation. You might try using a mix of charts, images, cartoons, text, and motion pictures or TV interviews to reinforce your material.

Charts are most effective to illustrate trends, establish relationships between two items, and make the subject visually easier to understand. Below are some of the types you can use.

1. Highlights to emphasize key points.

2. Time-sequence to show relationships over a period of time.

3. Organizational to show relationships between individuals, departments, or jobs.

4. Cause and Effect (spilled water near your keyboard spells disaster).

5. Flow Chart to reflect movement.

Cartoons are also welcome. They reinforce message points in a humorous way that increases retention. Beware of copyright violation, however. Many cartoonists are providing their work on the Internet and license it for a small fee. Some will even create cartoons to suit your program. A general search on your favorite Internet search engine will bring up several names.

Still Pictures and Video

If you are giving a talk at a retreat or an after dinner talk to a corporation, you might consider ways you can take still pictures or even live footage of the key members and use this in a humorous way in your presentation.

At the National Speakers Association Convention recently, at least a half-dozen speakers made effective use of weaving a live interview into their presentations. If you are presenting in a venue that provides hands-on technical support and equipment, short clips of video or film can be highly effective.

Working With Text

The easiest way to use PowerPoint is to use plain text, perhaps with a logo or simple image. This PowerPoint projected page of text (often called a slide) should be used the way you would use a sound bite: short, succinct, and to the point.

The slide should "snap" onto the screen and into the participant's mind, immediately reinforcing your core point with as few words as possible.

Effective Powerpoint Mandates

1. Focus on the audience, not your slides. Rehearse your Powerpoint privately and when delivering your presentation, look at your computer screen or notes, **not the slides.**

2. Rehearse in the room before the presentation and make sure all participants can see the visual.

3. Be certain that whatever slide you show reinforces a key point or injects humor in the presentation.

4. Use color, but not more than three colors per slide.

5. Write phrases, not complete sentences.

6. Use only one heading and font style per visual.

7. Use a parallel structure of words on each visual.

8. Incorporate text slides with charts and/or cartoons for variation.

9. Consider numbering key points rather than using bullets. This way, you can make a direct reference (i.e. look at point three.")

Another mistake many presenters commit with PowerPoint is to cram too much information on the slide. Ideally, you should use no more than three lines of text, each no more than three or four words. Images that reflect the concept are always a good idea.

The slide is a representation of the briefest outline possible.

The strongest "do" of all is to seriously qualify each visual before deciding to use it. When in doubt, leave it out. Too many cooks in the kitchen ruin the broth.

Flip Charts

Flip charts are fun to use and appropriate when you are presenting to less than twenty-five people. The advantages are that you can use the flip chart for interactive group exercises, and you can use it to list session objectives as they come up.

As we enter 2003, the flip chart as we know it is being replaced by a device that looks like a flip chart, but actually connects with a laptop computer. Whatever is written on the chart using special pens is conveyed to the computer, providing lasting documentation and material that can immediately be printed out for all participants.

Interactive Activities

As I mentioned earlier in the beginning of the chapter, interactive activities increase retention. Again, use your own judgment by analyzing the audience and the material to be covered to see if interactivity will add to the presentation. Most participants crave interactivity and role playing exercises. They are a great excuse to get up and move around. In my presentations, I usually use a flip chart to create a group mind mapping session. I also divide the audience into pairs or small groups and have them work on a short, five minute project together. You might try brainstorming activities that would be appropriate for the material you are presenting.

Props

Props are welcome at most presentations, but they must be appropriate. The best props are colorful, appear fun, and stimulate creativity. Arthur Hull, a national speaker and drum expert, really wowed attendees at a National Speaker's Convention by handing out colorful hollow tubes called "Boomwackers." By the end of the program, he had us create a symphony of sound to underscore his oratory theme of partnership and synergy. Other fun props can be a Super 8 ball, toys, and anything that adds a touch of whimsy while reinforcing your message.

Handouts

Do you collect handouts? You should. A good handout is easily worth the price of the course. It will contain online references, valuable resources, and key points of the talk you might have otherwise missed.

And most important for you who use presentations as a way to promote your business, book, services, or products, a very good handout will be kept literally forever. What better way for this potential target customer of yours to get a hold of you than to call the number on the handout?

However, most books on presentations advise against giving out a handout at the beginning of class, for fear that attendees will concentrate on the handout instead of the speaker. Perhaps these books were referring to a more passive audience than the ones I typically encounter. Today's attendees expect, even demand, a handout at the beginning of class. To be honest with you, I'm one of them. I take notes, but appreciate a handout for guidance.

So, then, what's the secret of having the attendees pay attention to you in class while satisfying their own need for a handout?

Here are some tips:

1. First, avoid the temptation to create a very structured handout, especially where time is concerned. Classes are very different, and you may find that you need to spend more time on a subject than you had planned. Most professional speakers create their talks using modules so that they can "add" or "subtract" a certain topic to make sure the class or seminar ends on time.

2. Create "teaser" handouts that have provocative titles and lines where attendees can fill in the information. As I explained earlier, attendees lean best with a combination of "hearing" the information, "seeing the information," and performing an exercise, even if the exercise is putting the concept physically on paper.

3. Tell attendees that at the end of class they should submit their business card, and you will email them a complete set of notes or your PowerPoint slides.

4. Send attendees to your web page, where you have the information/slides/notes uploaded for later viewing and reinforcement.

Key To Success: Practice

Practice is important for every presentation, but it's doubly important for a presentation with audio and/or visual material because the mechanics of handling audio-visual material sometimes can interfere with the presentation flow.

Rehearse the presentation with your audio-visual aids, preferably on videotape or audiotape. Simply rehearsing alone before a mirror is better than not rehearsing if audio and visual recording material is not available to you.

If you are able to record your presentation, you have the advantage of listening to it from the viewpoint of an audience member and find flaws that might otherwise escape you.

When you are ready, gather some co-workers or friends to hear your "practice presentation." Be certaom you give them an evaluation sheet that highlights what they liked best, what needs work, and so on. You also will want to invite commentary on the slides, illustrations, or other audiovisual material you used. Ask questions such as if they would have preferred more visual material, less visual material, etc., which relate to your presentation.

Collect the evaluation sheets and make adjustments in your final presentation based on the results of your practice sessions.

Setting Up the Room with Visual Aids

Since you will be setting up the room with aids, it's important to be early enough to set it up and test, especially in the venue is unfamiliar. Far in advance, get the phone number of people you may call in case of a technical conflict. There is always a chance you need an extension cord, a bulb, or some piece of equipment.

You will also want to test the equipment to make sure that all participants can see and there are no obstructions.

More Success Tips

1. Never use a visual aid before you have rehearsed with it and smoothed over transition points.

2. Be certain the aid is a help rather than a hindrance to communication. Remember, it must be clear and drive home your key message.

3. Don't show visual aids until you are ready to use them.

4. Speak to the audience, not the aid.

5. Use a pointer and stand to one side when discussing the aid.

6. Don't pass visual aids, either show them to the group at once or make them available after the presentation.

Summary:

☑ Visual aids help an audience retain information;

☑ Visual aids make the material come alive and infuses it with energy;

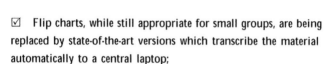

☑ Many types of data can be included in aids such as Microsoft Powerpoint;

☑ Flip charts, while still appropriate for small groups, are being replaced by state-of-the-art versions which transcribe the material automatically to a central laptop;

☑ Props are welcome but must be approrpiate;

☑ There are ways to distribute handouts that don't take focus from you as a presenter;

☑ Practicing with visual aids is essential;

☑ Assemble a group for feedback before your talk;

☑ Arrive early to set up the room.

Assignments:

1. The more varieties of aids you can incorporate in your talk, the higher the energy. Consider the different ways you can transmit your material (i.e. PowerPoint slides, handouts, pre-printed charts, motion pictures, samples or specimens, worksheets, exhibits).

2. While rehearsing alone for your next presentation, pay special attention to the way you handled the visual aids. Note specifically:

☑ Did you stop speaking to handle the aid?

☑ Did the effort of positioning the aid break your connection with the audience?

If you found yourself losing your connection to the audience as you adjusted your aids, practice these "joints" of the presentation, and give a rehersal in front of a group.

Create an evaluation sheet and questions that specifically relate to how you handled the aid.

Chapter 9
Networking with Confidence

In This Chapter You Will Learn

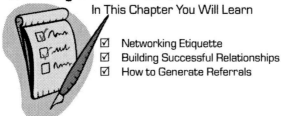

- ☑ Networking Etiquette
- ☑ Building Successful Relationships
- ☑ How to Generate Referrals

"The nearer you come into relation with a person, the more necessary do tact and courtesy become."

Oliver Wendell Holmes (1809 - 1894)

What is effective networking? In the best of all worlds, it's when you meet someone at a business or social event. who becomes a client or refers you to new clients or employers. Most often, a networking event is a fertile farmland for you to plant the seeds of future opportunity by positioning yourself as someone others need to know by a show of your energy, enthusiasm, authority and shared resources.

Networking is an activity that can take place between acts at the Opera, in the bleachers at a Little League game, or at a formal Chamber of Commerce event. Whether the meeting is social, business, or both, you would do well to observe some simple networking rules.

Approaching Formal Networking Events As Live Theater

Have you heard of *Tony and Tina's Wedding?* It's a live theatrical performance where the audience is invited to participate and interact with the actors. In their role as wedding guests, the audience enjoys a wedding feast with the "actors" and is encouraged to converse with them.

When you receive an invitation to a formal networking event sponsored by a trade organization or your local Chamber of

Commerce meeting, it is advantageous to consider the event a "performance." Realize in advance it is best if you take yourself out of your usual, everyday shell to meet and greet as many different people as possible.

Look Camera Ready

Have you noticed that newscasters on television always look "camera ready?" Their suits are clean and

pressed. Their appearance is neat and pulled together. Their smile is bright and they vibrate with energy. Most look directly into the camera as if they are looking only at you and are happy to see you.

Manifesting a newscaster's neat appearance and professional manner is a tall order, but a good role model to aspire to with regard to business in general and networking occasions specifically.

Mastering the skills of effective networking means that we must always be "camera ready" to make exciting new contacts whether we're stopping at the grocery store for a quart of milk or at a child's Little League game. Since we never know who is overhearing us or viewing our actions, we must always be polite, on good behavior, and neatly attired.

Radiate Positive Energy

You might consider effective networking as a positive energy exchange between two individuals in given moment of time and space. As you introduce yourself, smile, make eye contact, and try to radiate as much positive energy as you can muster. You never know where the interaction may lead, and you only have once chance to make that crucial first impression.

Networking Etiquette

"Do unto others as you would like to have done unto you."

We've all been appreciative and flattered when others go out of their way to be kind, helpful, and take an interest in us. Conversely, many of us have also felt slighted by those who couldn't see our true value.

Many, if not most, people are in a heightened state of self-conscious behavior when they attend a networking event, especially if they are alone. They feel that all eyes are on them, and are hyper-sensitive.

For this reason and others, it's a good idea to truly radiate good will, look them in the eye, and not single out "important people" you feel you need to meet. Everyone can be an asset to you with a positive endorsement, even if it is to add a "wow, she's great" when they hear your name mentioned in conversation.

Meeting and Greeting

Assume you are walking into a networking event alone, and everyone seems to know one another. What should you do? I usually look for a person who just arrived, extend my hand, and say hello. Sometimes, they are waiting for someone and are glad for the company. When their friend arrives, it's usually a good time to break off and continue to work the room, but every situation is different.

Should You Break In On Two Folks Together?

In a word, no. This is especially true if they seem to be engaged in an important conversation. Usually, it's okay to approach three people who look as if they are visibly being social, not whispering what appear to be trade secrets.

I often approach three strangers by venturing forth, waiting at the outskirts of the group, and wait to be included in. Sometimes, if I know the three all just met and the purpose for the meeting is to network, I will simply inject myself into the group with an introduction.

Breaking Up and Moving On Without Tears

Contrary to the lyrics of a popular song, breaking up is not hard to do. To not appear rude simply be honest. Don't say you are going to the rest room if your entire goal is to meet the important person at the other end of the room. Avoid breaking off by asking the other individual if you can refresh their drink — you will find yourself in the same situation when you return, and if you don't return, you will definitely appear rude.

Honesty is the best policy. Physically take a step backward, extend your hand to shake, and warmly vocalize how great it was to meet them and that you look forward to meeting them again soon. As you step back say something along the lines of "I'm sure you have many people to meet and I've taken enough of your time."

How much time is enough time before moving on? Seven to nine minutes is about right. After all, the objective of networking events is to "meet" the other individual, make a positive impression, exchange positive energy, and set the stage for future interaction if appropriate.

Be Polite To Everyone, Because Word Gets Around!

Some consider networking events a giant fishbowl of opportunity where one can swim around, looking for the "winning ticket" — that magical person who will somehow be our conduit to a better job or lucrative client.

It's true. Networking can be a great way to generate leads and business opportunities. But networking, like sales, is a game of numbers. The more events you attend and people you meet, the greater your opportunity.

Networking is also a game of energy. The more positive energy you project, the more positive events will come your way.

Energy is contagious. We've all met people who radiate the kind of positive energy that energizes us when we're around them. Some people are genuinely born with this positive energy. They have the kind of smile that literally does seem to light up a room. Others have trained themselves to acquire this energy and use it to energize themselves and others.

It's important to realize that networking events are "energy exchanges" in the fullest sense of the word. Even if the fundamental goal is to "get" new clients and contacts, it's important to give as well. For your own benefit, it behooves you to at least make the appearance of giving through the energy you project with helpful tips, and resources.

The reason "appearance" is so important is that even if you only meet a few people, you are being watched, judged, and analyzed. No matter how dark the room or crowded the event, people who can make or break your career are watching you. More important, they are listening to the comments of people you might have brushed off as inconsequential.

Gloria, a client, told me with shame that at one networking event she used the ladies room. Drying her hands at the sink, she noticed a woman next to her but didn't smile, say hello, or hold open the door as the woman followed her out. Imagine Gloria's surprise when the woman turned out to be the interviewer she'd face in the HR department of a new job she hoped to snare!

No words were exchanged between the women, but nonverbally, the HR woman felt Gloria snubbed her and was rude.

The Entire World is a Stage

The social world is filled with misunderstandings and misinterpretations. While it's important to be ourselves, we should also strive to be the best selves we can be.

If attending a networking event is similar to live theater, we should be like actors and rehearse expected lines in advance.

Key Points To Avoid

Too often, people ramble when introduced to others. They overtake the conversation, speaking too long about their business and interest, and not sprinkling the conversation with "you magic."

By "you magic" I am referring to the "magic" that happens when you use the word "you." You've heard it said that people enjoy talking about themselves, and this is especially true when the other person seems sincere in their interest. By showing an interest in others, you make yourself magnetically attractive to them.

Another behavior to avoid is chatting with one individual too long. Yes, you may be relieved to have found someone so you're not feeling conspicuous, but understand that the purpose of the event is networking. Often, the person you are chatting with may be too polite to break off the conversation, leaving the honor to you.

What Not To Say

You will want to stockpile some "template phrases" you can adapt for various networking occasions. The most important rule is that everything you say has a pleasant, energizing ring.

You've known people who are complainers, finding fault with everything from the weather to their health. Avoid this! Any negative statement brings the energy level down. Most dangerous are negative words. Negativity can be "associated" with you simply

by virtue of the comment you left behind.

The most egregious caution is speaking negatively about anyone. This can return and haunt you for years to come. It can ruin your reputation, hurt innocent people, and cost you your credibility while damaging your business and career. As mother said, "if you can't say something nice about someone, don't say anything at all."

On equal footing to being negative about others is repeating gossip. It doesn't matter whether the gossip is positive or negative in tone. Jane, a friend of mine who is careful to always be positive and upbeat, revealed she once mentioned in passing that she heard a certain individual was romantically involved with another, thinking the story perfectly innocent and neutral. Two days later, she was mortified to receive an email from the individual in question, begging her to stop telling the story because it just wasn't true and would hurt his present partner. "There and then," Jane told me, "I swore never to repeat any gossip. Period."

Phrases to Stockpile

So, what should you say? As in every presentation, forethought is key. One statement you will always need is a "self introduction." It should last about 7 seconds and express what you do in the most vibrant, colorful, dynamic way possible.

For example, I tell people "I'm Marisa D'Vari, and I help you build brand, buzz, and business through presentation skills and media positioning."

A bond specialist can say: "I help you bond with their future via safe investments."

A defense lawyer can say: "if you're ever falsely accused of stealing from the cookie jar, I'm your man."

A financial planner can say: "I help you and your family sleep soundly at night."

A hairdresser can say, "I take care of your loose ends."

The bottom line is to be as colorful and bold as you dare.

An accountant who introduces herself by saying "I turn loose coins into millions" telegraphs several things. First, the fact that she has a sense of humor and promises to be a "fun" person to chat with.

Second, the bold statement provokes a follow-up question such as "Wow! How?!" If she had answered with a typical "oh, I'm an accountant" she would come across as immediately dull, wouldn't she? The creative statement articulated above gives her color and personality. It also makes her seem as if she enjoys her job and the challenges that go along with it.

Consider yourself. If you had a choice of hiring or recommending an accountant, would you go for the woman who says, "Oh, I'm an accountant" as if it's a job she's forced into? Or an accountant who basks in the fact she saves her clients so much money?

No matter how serious your occupation, try to devise a way that reveals what you do for a living and can provide a spot of fun and color in an otherwise bland world.

Talking to Strangers

In France, people feel comfortable striking up a conversation with strangers who are assembled under "one roof," such as a cocktail party or networking event. The feeling is that since they have all been invited by the host, the "roof" serves as their introducer in the host's place. Author Marcel Proust often has characters meet one another in his novels using this way, presumably to cut out extra characters who'd otherwise clutter the storyline.

So, how do you introduce yourself? I usually spot someone and either extend my hand, or if we're waiting in line at the buffet or cocktails, simply say my name and make a casual comment.

A casual comment is a remark you make about the weather, the group or gathering, or the food at the location. The only rule is that it must be positive (i.e. "golly, we really need all this wonderful rain!") and spoken in a voice that positions you as a fun, positive person to talk to.

When you receive a response, a good idea is to compliment something the other individual is wearing — which is also a great approach on its own.

One of my most memorable stories is that of meeting networking guru Susan Roane in the ladies room at the Book Expo America (BEA) convention in Chicago, which coincided with the National Speakers Association (NSA) that year. I was a book author and frankly, had never met a professional speaker.

But Susan, being the master networker she is, automatically smiled at me as I applied lipstick. "Is that a St. John suit?" she asked. "I love St. John -- so great to pack since I travel all the time."

"Oh, what do you do?" I asked.

Susan explained that she was a speaker, and when I expressed interest into knowing what a speaker did, she took me by the hand and dragged me over to a luncheon for NSA members, introduced me to a few people. I quickly learned more, joined, and have been a happy NSA member for the last several years.

Commenting on Appearance

Has anyone ever commented on your briefcase or handbag? What about your ring or other item of jewelry? Everyone has been complimented on some aspect of what they are wearing at one time or another, and usually the compliment is heartfelt. I would caution you to steer away from anything too personal.

Others are flattered when we comment on something they obviously take pride in. A certain sect of women, mostly involved in fashion or a "glamour" profession, take pride in their shoes. If you are also in this field and appreciate the design of a woman's shoe, your notice will be greatly appreciated.

Jewelry is a far safer bet. Almost everyone has a fun, colorful story they enjoy retelling when complimented on their jewelry. PR maven Dorothy Molstad wears gold and ruby slipper earrings,

because she is a "Dorothy" from "Kansas." Many people design their own jewelry, or have an emotional attachment to jewelry they inherited.

Compliments are appropriate, only if they are heartfelt and sincere. Therefore try to identify an item that others might not notice, because this singles you out and makes you appear unique.

Business Cards

Just as you must appear professionally dressed at a networking event, your business cards should look fresh and well pressed as well.

Take a look at your card right now. This card is conceivably offered to a dozen potential clients a day. Is the card appropriately dressed? Do you approve of its appearance? Does it reflect the value you feel that you and your services are worth? Your card, after all, will reflect your image long after you are gone.

Some people innocently assume that a business card is simply a vehicle for contact information. But consider that your business card is kept long after you and your expensively attired appearance is long gone. Unlike a brochure or bulky material, people tend to hang on to your business card and many keep it for years. Vicki Donlan, publisher of *Women's Business Boston*, not only keeps cards she receives but she actually writes information on them, recording the place she met the cardholder and ideas on how they might do future business together.

Consider the image your card will have when seen against many others, especially cards of high quality. Will it stand up to the competition? If you use a company card and feel it's not up to snuff, talk to the president and explain why changes are necessary. If you are an entrepreneur now realizing the importance of cards, begin collecting cards and comparing them to one another. Which ones reflect quality? Why?

It's a good idea to put your business cards in many different places so you will always have them at hand. This includes the pocket of your coat(s), all of your purses or briefcases, your wallet, your palm pilot holder, and anywhere else you can name.

Beyond having your business card with you, you will want to have it handy so that you don't have to fumble around looking for it, especially if you're holding a glass of wine, a hors d'oeurvres, or other material.

At trade shows and conferences, my trick is to put a small stack inside the plastic container that holds your nametag. That way, cards are always at the ready, and you will have a place to put the cards of others as well. At events where you know you must deliver several cards in a short period of time, for example, during the five minute interval at a Chamber of Commerce networking event or "Leads meeting," you may find it helpful to carry a small stack of cards discreetly in your pocket.

Of course, the most elegant way to carry cards is in a case. Similar to your pen, your case should be the finest you can afford. People WILL notice a tarnished or scratched metal case, so be wary of this if you are about to buy one. If you already have a case that is tarnished and you are hoping that no one will notice, why not consider a new one.

Some books are dedicated completely to the ceremony of handing out a business card. Since a card is an extension of yourself, treat the cards of others with equal respect. Most people are honored if you write on the back of their card in order to make an important note, but consider that since the card is an extension of another individual, this action can be perceived negatively. It is better to practice to first show respect by looking into the eyes of the other, smiling, and ask if they mind if you make a notation on their card.

Building Successful Relationships

We attend networking events for a variety of reasons, and would love to "get lucky" and meet the key person who can become our biggest client or referral of clients the first go-round. But just as advertisers know that consumers must see your name seven times before they buy, you must "build" a relationship step by step.

Be Seen as a Connector

Chances are, there is someone in your social circle who knows everyone and everything. They know the best hotel in St. Tropez and the best restaurant in every major city, along with the name of the General Manager.

In his book *The Anatomy of Buzz*, Emanuel Rosen suggests that this "connector" is crucial to the success or failure of any venture of interest to a specific market. In his book *The Tipping Point*, author Malcolm Gladwell singles out history's Paul Revere as a connector. Revere was famous for shouting that the British were coming — but also held positions including that of Suffolk County coroner, health officer of Boston, key member of the streetlight committee, and founder of the Massachusetts Mutual Fire Insurance Company.

Connectors have power. They are both made and born.

Qualities of a Connector

☑   Connectors are masterful networkers in any situation. They know how to work a room with sincerity, but also a purpose.

☑   Connectors enjoy great "buzz" — people are always saying positive things about them because of the impression they make.

☑   Connectors are giving, yet well aware of the laws of energy exchange, which mandates that one must also receive.

How to be a Connector

Becoming a connector is a process that happens one step at a time. The first step is realizing one can point themselves on a "connector's track." This means that you should look into joining suitable trade organizations where you can connect with others.

The second step is to volunteer and take responsibility for actions you undertake.

It's been said that if you need something done quickly and well, ask a busy person. In this way, you will find that the more you do the more you can do.

Stay In Touch

To spread the word about the British, Paul Revere had to take a wild midnight ride across New England. Today, we just have to get on the Internet and send an email, an ezine, or a link to an article that may be of interest to someone we want to connect with. We can even accomplish this offline, with a phone call suggesting a referral or mail an envelope containing a tear-out of an article or even a short, handwritten note saying how great it was to meet them.

By staying in touch and giving people links, articles, or items of interest, we are marking ourselves clearly in their mind as memorable.

Generating Referrals

At its core, the purpose at any networking event is create awareness of who you are and what you do. We might not meet our ideal prospect at a networking event, but we have 100% chance of meeting someone who can ultimately refer us to our prospect.

Millions of people credit referrals with building a lucrative business. But remember, referrals are a two-way street. They are a form of energy exchange. You only get as good as you give.

Develop a Referral Mindset

Networking with a referral mindset does not mean that you race around the room, shoving your business card in people's faces and asking them how they can help you. The process is simple, but best viewed as a series of steps.

First, identify a target industry. Look closely at the networking events, the different representative organizations, and the publications. Make yourself visible to this group on paper by contributing articles to their publications and become involved in at the organizational level by serving on various committees.

Always position yourself as a connector when speaking to a potential referral, strategizing on how you can best serve them and their interests. Soon, you will begin to get referrals.

When you do receive a valuable referral, two things must happen. First, always give much more than was expected to the client, and be sure to ask the client for referrals and a testimonial.

Second, acknowledge the person who referred you with a handwritten note of heartfelt thanks and perhaps a small gift.

Who Do You Already Know?

When developing a referral mindset, start with fans, friends, and satisfied clients already growing in your garden. Who have you served who has thanked you for your value?

Protocol and Dealing With Sticky Situations

Do you have a pet peeve when you meet new people? Many people feel uncomfortable when others stand too close. Respect the personal space of others, since violating this rule is a quick way to alienate people who may have been helpful to you.

Use your own judgment when addressing a new acquaintance by their first name, especially if they are older than you. Usually, people will quickly say "call me Ted" or whatever their first name happens to be.

Keep networking conversation polite and superficial. Don't get too personal. Do you remember the E.F. Hutton commercial, when the room suddenly went quiet? During a conversation, if you feel a question may be inappropriate, imagine the room suddenly going quiet and everyone listening in. Do you still want to ask?

Networking As a Way of Life

At its core, networking is a way of living your professional and social life. None of us exist in a vacuum, and if we are in business, we rely on others to he us mentally, spiritually, and in business.

Above all else, realize that networking is an exchange of energy.

Make certain that you radiate positive energy, and clearly expect positive results to attract like-minded individuals.

Summary:

☑ Approach networking events as live theater;

☑ Look "camera ready";

☑ Radiate positive energy

☑ Network with etiquette;

☑ Limit interactions to 7 minutes;

☑ Remember the world is your stage;

☑ Bring good quality business cards;

☑ Become a connector.

Assignments:

1. Decide to secretly impersonate a confident character from a film at your next networking event. Be yourself, but radiate that chosen character's confidence. Does it work for you? It can be a very effective confidence-building tool.

2. Stand before a mirror and take stock of yourself. Do you like your image? Can it be improved with a wardrobe change representative of the new you, even if it's one suit? Women, consider updating your look with a complimentary makeover at the cosmetics counter.

3. Decide in advance to break into a threesome at your next networking event. Visualize them welcoming you in your mind before you take the action. See great things happening as a result.

4. Since you know you must break off with someone after nine minutes, even if you are having a great interaction, plan how you will do it before ever arriving at the event. Remember, take a step back and make a polite statement. What will you say?

5. Walk into the event knowing that every action counts, because people "see" you when you don't see them - and they talk. Be polite to everyone.

6. Consider reworking your business card if this is an option for you.

7. Resolve to send a thank you note or email to everyone who's card you collect at the end of the event.

Chapter 10
Video Conferencing Success

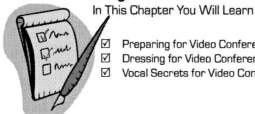

In This Chapter You Will Learn

☑ Preparing for Video Conferencing
☑ Dressing for Video Conferencing
☑ Vocal Secrets for Video Conferencing

"In the future, everyone will have 15 minutes of fame."
Andy Warhol (1928 - 1987)

In today's world, travel is both difficult and expensive. Technology has improved to the point where executives can make very successful presentations via video conferencing.

So, you might ask, what are the key differences between "live" and video presentations?

When individuals meet face to face, many nonverbal messages are exchanged at a subconscious level. These messages are often what motivate buyers to "buy" into what you have to sell. When we present via video conferencing, we must do our best to really "reach" the audience by using all the tools available to us, our gestures, our dress, and our voice.

The objective of this chapter is not to explain the "mechanics" of setting up for a video conference, but instead, how to mesmerize your audience via "video presentation skills."

Appearance

In conjunction with a rehearsed presentation, *appearance takes on a new highlighted role.*

Many of the "rules" for video conferencing are similar to that of television.

Appearance is mostly limited to the "shoulders up" so the **concept of shape** takes on a new role. The objective should be a **smooth, yet clearly defined shape.**

- **Shoulders are key**
    - Suits should have clearly defined shoulders, preferably padded.

    - Women's suits come in a variety of untraditional styles which may be fine. Beware of:

        - A suit that gaps or bunches up near the chest when sitting.
        - A suit and blouse that is lower cut.
        - A suit/top that does not look "smooth" in a seated position.
        - Colors that can "vibrate" on screen including:
            - all white;
            - all red;
            - small patterns (checks, plaids).

- **Hair gives shape to the face**

    Your shoulders and your hair frame your body on the screen. Consider your hair style and how you will wear it that day.

    - Consider gel to smooth frizzy hair.
    - Keep longer hair out of your face.
    - Be aware of touching your hair.
    - Be certain color is fresh.

Video Conference grooming for women

- Keep makeup simple.
- Keep lipstick off teeth.
- Eyeliner can help others focus on your eyes.

Video Conference grooming for both sexes

- Nails should look maintained.
- Avoid distracting nail habits.
- Assume you are under constant observation.

Accessories

- Beware of jewelry that will "flash" on camera.
- Eyeglasses should be glare-resistant.
- Beware of jewelry that can make noise.
- Small, conservative jewelry if worn is best.

Posture

Posture is almost equal to appearance in terms of importance. In video conferencing and on television, you must look "involved" and "at attention."

- Use visualization to imagine the string of a powerful balloon holding your head at the center.

- Keep shoulders straight and squared.

- Your chair can have a positive/negative effect on your posture. What kind of chair will be in the room? Each requires a different posture in order to televise well.

- If your jacket is long enough, sit on the bottom to reduce bunching.

Gestures & Eye Contact

- Gestures will give added life to your presentation, but they should be smaller and more controlled.

- Your image is two dimensional, so a smile is more important.

- Beware that television will highlight any irritation, so keep any negative emotions in check.

- Look at the camera lens as if you were looking at a key member of your audience, speak directly to them.

Vocal Variety

Vocal Variety is of key importance. As is the case in giving a presentation to a live audience, you must use your voice to highlight, underline, and bring attention to key concepts.

Team Connection

- Radiate a sense of team connection.
- When a team member is speaking, nod along encouragingly even if you do not think you are being televised.
- In some situations, you may wish to consider if it is appropriate to announce your name before speaking. This serves to identify you as well as giving the camera (in certain situations) to move to you.

Distractions

Noises that you may not notice in a personal meeting can become distracting in a video conference. Avoid:

- Tapping on a desk.
- Whispering to others.

- Shuffling paper.
- Avoid unnecessary movements (rocking in chair, moving from side to side).

Utilizing Vocal Variety to Enhance Your Message

When your objective is to convey information to others, you must consider every "tool" available to you as a communicator.

Your content may be rich, but it **represents only 7%** of what an audience understands as a result of your talk.

Consider two common, high information formats of information: html, and the still photo. When you view the html of a high content web page, you "get" **the mass of valuable information**, but are you able to clearly see the author's vision? Pictures are conveyed via code, and ideas are distorted by even more code.

We all know the power of still images, but **when these still images "move" in the form of documentaries**, with *music, sound, charts*, and so forth, our understanding of the subject is more complete.

Typesetters realize the importance of **headlines, subheads, paragraphs, and a mix of short and long sentences, periods, and exclamation marks.**

As presenters, we must use the power of our voice to mimic the typesetter's art, and communicate our ideas more clearly to our audience.

Increasing Audience Understanding, Engagement, & Recall

As the world's greatest orators and evangelists have tapped into the power of "breaking up" complex thoughts to enhance audience retention.

They have tapped into the knowledge of typesetters and composers of classical music to enhance audience understanding, engagement, and recall.

As a presenter, your most powerful tool is not the strength of your content but the power of your voice to motivate the audience and make them want to "hear" your message.

Today's celebrity chefs know they must "dazzle the eye" before they can tempt the palate. Elaborate amuse bouche are presented to dinners in order to create interest in the five-star meal that will follow.

Some chefs take the concept even further than dazzling the eye with a colorful, delectable amuse bouche. They further stir the patron's hunger with an alluring scent to increase interest in their creation.

As a presenter, you must use your own "tools" to create a hunger for your audience to hear your message.

Knock Before Entering

Door to door salespeople knock before bursting into your home to blurt out their message.

Resentment is building against email marketers who insert themselves into your "inbox" without permission.

Audiences have expressed their permission in hearing your message by appearing in your audience, but they still need to be seduced.

You seduce an audience to listen to your message by tapping into the power of your voice.

Voice Dynamics

Great composers are well aware of the power they yield. In any classical composition, the careful listener can hear the **instruments speak, whine, cry, lament, laugh, reflect, become melancholy, energize, and otherwise mimic human emotion as conveyed through voice.**

Listeners may not be aware of the core issues the instruments (or, rather, the composer) may have been dealing with, but the sounds are so emotional that listeners tap into that emotion, and subconsciously take in the "message" that is being conveyed, even though they may not understand it on a conscious level.

Composers have instruments mimic human emotion through a variety of methods. One method is intensity. For human beings interested in using their voice more effectively, "intensity" reflects the tension of your voice and how you emphasize words.

Consider the sentence below:

*Vocal variety is the **only way** to keep your audience engaged and increase understanding.*

When you select a word or phrase to intensify, you can change the meaning of the sentence. Stress "vocal variety" and you make this phrase stands out. Stress "only way" and this phrase stands out.

Realize that you must play "maestro" with your voice, and use the composer's tools to add power to your message.

Inflection

In the world of music, composers have instruments "speak" louder, faster, slower, or softer to aid the communication sent to the audience. Composers have instruments "pause" for short or long periods of time, and can have their "voice" go up or down for brief scores.

Inflection is a great aid when it comes to enhancing vocal variety in your presentations. You can understand its power more clearly when you consider how music composers and typesetters use similar tools to make text and music more understandable.

The Pause

The pause is a tool with incredible power. Superficially, it makes you appear to be more "professorial" and enhances your credibility. As a tool, it enables your audience to catch up with you, process your observations, and map them to their own experience.

It is said that nature abhors a vacuum, and many speakers become anxious when they leave "empty space" in their presentation. A pause that might seem an "eternity" to you is very short when you see yourself on video tape.

More important, when you train yourself to pause, you can obliterate the need to add "filler" words to your presentation.

Symbols for Vocal Variety

Across are some symbols you can use to mark up your speech. Simply print out your talk in a large type with narrow margins, so that you would only be reading four inches in the middle of your page.

Look at each word and determine if the word should be emphasize. If so, determine in which manner, and mark with the appropriate symbol.

It is all about Communication

Effective communicators are made, not born. Give yourself definitive goals, and time to practice.

Join a Toastmasters group in your city.

Follow the advice in this book, and videotape regularly.

All best wishes for your success!

< Louder or Faster

> Soft or Slower

~~ Emphasize (mark under words)

//Long Pause

/ Short Pause (mark between words)

^ Tie together

- Voice up (mark above words)

‾ Voice down (mark below words)

Deg.Com Communications offers a wide vareity of learning materials to help your professional performance, including books, audio tapes, and video tapes.

To view the entire list and purchase online, please visit our web site.

www.deg.com

Our web site also has many free articles and resources for your convenience.

Marisa D'Vari welcomes your questions and comments on this book. You can reach her at mdvari@deg.com